THE WORLD OF FOOD

China

The World of Food

❦

China

❦

by Kenneth Lo

THOMAS Y. CROWELL COMPANY
New York / Established 1834

Kenneth Lo was born in China and was educated at Yenching University in Peking. He has had a distinguished career in the Chinese foreign service, as a publisher, and as an author and lecturer on current affairs in China as well as on Chinese food and cooking. He has written for many publications including *The Times* of London and *The Observer*, and is the author of *Cooking the Chinese Way*.

Published by The World Publishing Company
Published simultaneously in Canada
by Nelson, Foster & Scott Ltd.

First printing–1973

Copyright © 1973 by The Hamlyn Publishing Group, Ltd.
All rights reserved
ISBN 0-529-04863-9
Library of Congress catalog card number: 73-78426
Printed in the United States of America

Project Director: Peter V. Ritner
Associate Project Director and Editor-In-Chief: Richard M. Beebe
Associate Editor: Mary Lee Allingham

Creative Director and Designer: Milton Charles
Assistant to Creative Director: Terry McKee
Illustrations: Ron Le Hew

Production Manager: Bernard Kass

ACKNOWLEDGMENTS
British Consulting Editor: Katie Stewart
American Consulting Editor: Ann Seranne
Liaison Editor: Audrey Ellis
Photographs by Eric Carter

WORLD PUBLISHING
TIMES MIRROR

Contents

Fukien 100

Southwest China 112

Canton 122

Before You Begin

For thousands of years, most Chinese peasants have been poor; Chinese cooking is based on thousands of years of experience learning to utilize every scrap. Fuel—taken for granted in the West—was regarded almost as an ingredient by the Chinese because of its scarcity; they gathered and burned bits of kindling, twigs, leaves—anything that was available. They also developed cooking methods that used as little fuel as possible: food is cut into small, uniform pieces before cooking, enabling everything to cook quickly and evenly over a minimum of fuel.

So important is Chinese food preparation that apprentice cooks, who traditionally studied for three years, would use two and one-half of them learning to cut. Perhaps the most important basic concept is the separation of *preparation* and actual *cooking* (which usually takes five minutes or less). The first must be done before the second is begun.

These distinctive characteristics of cooking influence the form of the meal itself. In the West, meals are built around a main dish (a whole fowl, roast beef, or other big cut of meat) with separately prepared vegetables and salad. Chinese meals consist of dishes that mix meat (or poultry or seafood) and vegetables (usually the main part), all precut and eaten with chopsticks. The number of different dishes depends on the number of guests, who simply help themselves to as much or as little as they please. Noodles and rice take the place of the Western potatoes or bread.

We suggest that the reader introduce himself gradually to this style of cooking. Start, for instance, by substituting a Chinese vegetable dish for one of your standard ones (along with the main meal you would ordinarily prepare). Next time, select a meat or chicken dish from the recipes here. Most Chinese meat, chicken, or fish dishes are combined with vegetables, so you can omit a vegetable from your regular menu.

Chinese food, properly prepared, is not only delicious—it is a healthful cuisine. It is high in protein (the soybean is used extensively in sauce and oil forms), low in calories (little bread is eaten), and low in fat (no butter or milk).

We have tried to select recipes whose ingredients are readily obtainable in most Western cities; available substitutes are suggested for hard-to-get items. However, before you turn to the recipes themselves, we suggest you read the following glossary to become acquainted with ingredients and cooking terms used in this book, particularly those that may be unfamiliar.

BASIC CHINESE INGREDIENTS

1   bean curd
2   water chestnuts
3   dried tangerine peel
4   red bean-curd cheese
5   fermented brown beans
6   dried Chinese
       mushrooms
7   winter bamboo shoots
8   wood-ears
9   fermented black beans
10 brown rock sugar
11 bamboo shoots
12 ginger root
13 litchis
14 lotus root
15 chili peppers
16 sea cucumber
17 Chinese salted cabbage
18 bean sprouts
19 egg noodles
20 wheat-flour noodles
21 Chinese cabbage
22 Chinese ham
23 transparent pea-starch
       noodles
24 rice stick noodles

Glossary

aniseed, or anise: the fruit of a small plant of the parsley family. The dried seeds are used as a flavoring agent. They should be stored in tightly sealed containers in a dry place.

bamboo shoots: ivory-colored shoots of tropical bamboo, eaten more for their crunchy texture than their subtle taste. They are available canned, either whole or in large pieces packed in water or brine. Bamboo shoots should be rinsed thoroughly in cold water before using. They will keep covered with water in a tightly sealed container in the refrigerator for at least a week if the water is changed every few days.

If fresh or canned bamboo shoots are unavailable, any crunchy, coarse-textured vegetable without too distinctive a flavor will approximate the texture but

not the flavor of bamboo shoots—hard cabbage, cauliflower stems, celery hearts, or kohlrabi.

bean curd: small squares of soy bean puree. It is an unusual, soft, spongy custard, creamy in color, highly nutritious, and widely used in China. Its own flavor is slight, but it absorbs and complements that of other foods. It may be cooked with almost any meat, fish, or vegetable; it is also used in soups. Bean curd is available either fresh or dried. Fresh bean curd may be kept covered with water in a tightly sealed jar in the refrigerator for a week if the water is changed every few days. Dried does not require refrigeration if it is kept tightly wrapped and used within a few months.

bean-curd cheese (Chinese red cheese): a salty, strong-tasting, fermented derivative of bean curd. It has no equivalent in flavor. It may be bought canned in a red

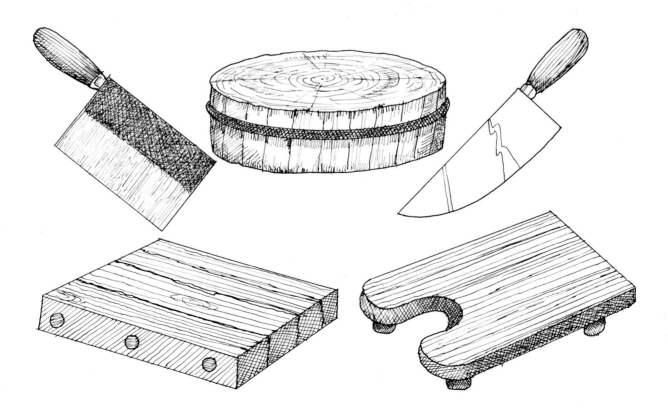

sauce and will keep in a covered jar in the refrigerator for several weeks. Mash the cubes before using.

beans, fermented black (black bean sauce): small preserved soy beans which are very salty. They usually come dried and must be soaked and mashed before using. If unavailable, add extra salt or soy sauce to the recipe.

beans, fermented brown (brown bean sauce): a thick and spicy paste, which is made from fermented yellow beans, flour, and salt. The beans are cooked before using. It may be used as an alternative to fermented black beans for frying and cooking with meats. It is available in small jars or cans. As a substitute use brown soy jam or additional salt.

bean paste, red: a sweetened puree of red beans which is used for stuffing, steamed pastries, and other sweet dishes. As a substitute use finely chopped dates.

bean sprouts: the sprouts or shoots of mung peas, they are crunchy in texture and combine well with other vegetables and meat. They may be bought fresh, canned, or frozen. Fresh ones should be stored in the refrigerator in a tightly sealed container filled with water. Change the water daily.

blanch: to plunge food into boiling water to soften, precook, partially cook, or to remove or reduce too strong a taste.

brown soy jam (brown soy paste): a thick paste made from fermented soy beans, it is basically the same as soy jam except for the color. If unavailable, the following preparation may be used as a substitute. Add 4 parts light soy sauce to 3 parts baked beans, and 1 part grated cheese. Mash and heat together over low heat until volume is reduced by one-third.

cabbages: *Chinese cabbage:* an extremely versatile and popular vegetable, which has long smooth white stalks and large crinkly dark-green leaves. It requires little cooking and has a delicate flavor. As a substitute use heart of Savoy cabbage or heart of celery.

celery cabbage: a crisp vegetable resembling a cross between romaine lettuce, celery, and cabbage. It has firm, tightly packed vertical leaves which are pale yellow with light-green tips. As a substitute use young celery, Swiss chard, or Savoy cabbage.

salted cabbage: the cabbages that are salted are green. They are generally salted using 1 part salt (in weight) to 12 parts cabbage, and then dried in the sun or a very low oven. Sometimes hot pepper is added. Salted cabbage is used with meat as a flavoring agent. It must be soaked in warm water, then rinsed in several changes of cold water before using.

mustard cabbage: similar in taste to broccoli, this dark-green vegetable has tightly packed scalloped leaves. It is similar in both size and texture to a small head of cabbage.

pickled Szechwan cabbage (Szechwan salted cabbage): hot and salty, this usually comes in small cans. It is used sliced or chopped in cooking meats, intensifying the flavor of the meats.

chili peppers: small red peppers, usually no more than 3 inches long, and shaped like an irregular horn. They are extremely hot in taste (probably the hottest vegetable in existence). The white seeds are usually discarded. Chili peppers often come dried, in which case they are even hotter. They are often fried to impregnate oil with their hotness. This oil is then used to cook meats and vegetables. When dried chili peppers are fried in oil, they give it a red color: this oil is called *chili oil* and is sometimes used—mixed with soy sauce—as a dip at the table. These peppers are used very sparingly. They may be purchased loose. Green and yellow chili peppers are occasionally available.

Chinese cabbage: *See* cabbages.

Chinese ham: The two best hams in China are the Yunnan ham and the Ching Hua ham. They are usually available sliced in cans. A good substitute is Smithfield ham—the redder its color, the more similar it is to the Chinese variety.

Chinese noodles: similar to spaghetti, particularly the threadlike vermicelli. The Italian products make good substitutes if Chinese noodles cannot be found. Chinese noodles come in four varieties.

egg noodles: yellow in color, egg noodles are often precooked, requiring only a short period of simmering in boiling water to loosen up before they are stir-fried, cooked in sauce, or added to soups. Dried egg noodles may be kept several weeks if tightly sealed in plastic bags and placed in the refrigerator.

rice stick (rice-flour) noodles: whiter in color than wheat-flour noodles, these come in straight fine strands, about 8 inches long. They are often cooked with wood-ears, mushrooms, meats, or seafood.

transparent pea-starch noodles: made from ground mung peas, they are white and opaque when raw and transparent after a period of soaking or simmering in water. This variety does not become soft and mushy when cooked, yet they absorb an enormous amount of broth or gravy. Unlike other noodles, they are never eaten alone—they are always cooked with meat, gravy, soup, or vegetables. Soak in warm water for a few minutes before using to prevent absorbing excessive liquid from the prepared dish.

wheat-flour noodles: looking like spaghetti, and made largely from the same ingredients, these form the staple diet of the northern Chinese. When cooked, they should be soft outside but still firm inside.

chopsticks: called "quick little boys" in Chinese, they are bamboo sticks used in pairs for cooking and eating. To hold, place a chopstick between the thumb and forefinger (about $\frac{2}{3}$ up from the small, or round, end) and hold it in place by bending the thumb over it; this chopstick maintains a relatively fixed position. The second chopstick, held between the end of the thumb and the forefinger, is free to move, supported by the middle finger. The tips should be even with each other. Pieces of food are held between the tips; rice is pushed from the raised rice bowl.

coriander (seeds): a musky-smelling herb, the dried seeds of which are used as a flavoring in meat, pickles, and pastry. The seeds are sold whole or ground. Store in tightly sealed containers in a dry place.

coriander (leaves): sold as Chinese parsley in some stores. The leaves have a pungent flavor and will keep for a week if stored, unwashed, in a plastic bag in the refrigerator.

doilies: similar in appearance to pancakes, except thinner and drier, these are made without eggs and heated without fat. Thin ordinary pancakes may be substituted.

Makes about 1½ dozen
1½ cups all-purpose flour
⅔ cup boiling water
3 tbs. sesame oil

Place the flour in a bowl. Slowly pour in the boiling water and gradually work to a warm dough. Knead gently for 1 to 2 minutes; then let stand for 10 minutes.

Shape the dough into a roll 2 inches in diameter. Cut the roll into ½-inch-thick slices. Brush one side of each slice with sesame oil and lay another slice on top of it with the oiled surfaces together. Roll the double piece out from the center on a lightly floured working surface until it spreads out to a pancake with a diameter of about 5 inches. Make as many pancakes as the dough allows. Heat a large, flat, heavy, ungreased skillet or omelet pan over low heat. When quite hot, place the pancake in the pan. Rotate the pan above the heat so the cooking is even. When the pancake starts to bubble, turn it over. After 2 or 3 minutes of heating on each side, pull each double piece of dough apart into separate slices. Fold each piece into a half circle on the side brushed with sesame oil. Pile the doilies on a plate and place in a steamer for 10 minutes, steaming before bringing them to the table. In China, such doilies are called "thin cakes" *(Po Bin)*.

dried Chinese mushrooms: brownish-black in color with a stronger flavor and firmer texture than fresh mushrooms. Clean them by rinsing in cold water; then soak in warm water for 20 to 30 minutes before using. The mushroom water itself makes an excellent flavoring agent. Soaked mushrooms may be kept several days if drained, wrapped in aluminum foil, and refrigerated. If dried Chinese mushrooms are unavailable, dried mushrooms from other regions may be used.

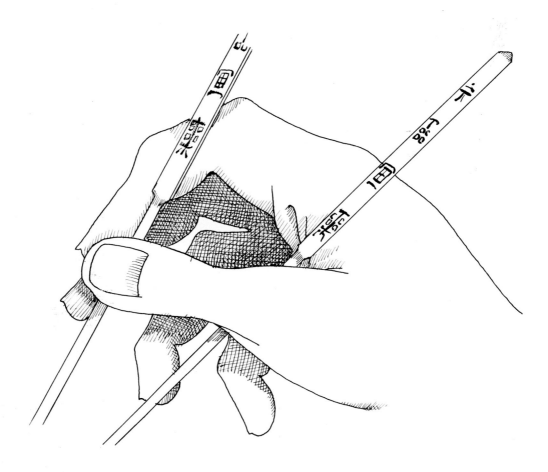

dried tangerine peel (Mandarin orange peel): used only in small quantities because the dried peel is stronger in flavor than fresh. If commercially unavailable, prepare it by drying fresh peel in a 250° oven for 3 hours. Turn the heat off and let stand in the oven overnight. Dried peel is usually soaked for 30 to 45 minutes before using.

dry mustard: the ground and powdered seeds of the mustard plant. This product is available in most supermarkets and should be stored in tightly sealed containers in a dry place.

fatback: the strip of fat cut from the back of a hog carcass, usually cured by dry-salting.

five-spice powder: a strong, fragrant powder consisting of star anise, anise pepper, fennel, cloves, and cinnamon. It is extremely pungent and should be used sparingly. Allspice may be used as a substitute.

frying: *deep-frying:* Food to be deep-fried is put in a wire basket and submerged in a pot of boiling oil or fat.

dry-frying: to fry without oil. Flour is sometimes browned by this method.

quick stir-frying (quick-frying): One of the most commonly employed and distinctive methods of Chinese cooking is *Ch'ao*, or quick stir-frying. The technique involves high heat, a minimal amount of oil, very short cooking time, and constant stirring. The food is usually cut into small pieces of equal size to facilitate even cooking. Seasoning and sauces are sometimes added and adjusted during the brief cooking. Often the foods to be cooked together are stir-fried separately first, then combined just before serving. This is necessary when the different foods require different cooking times. Another reason for separate cooking is the need to keep individual flavors distinct until final assembly. As a rule, unhydrogenated vegetable oils (such as soy bean, corn, or peanut) that can stand high temperatures without burning are used for quick stir-frying. Chicken fat is used in delicate cooking—to sauté vegetables, for example. For ordinary cooking, lard is sometimes used.

The wok, the traditional Chinese frying pan, is particularly useful in quick stir-frying. It is deep with steeply sloped sides. Its shape concentrates the heat, requires little oil, and facilitates the crucially important stirring and tossing of the cooking food. The implements used for stirring are a *siou hok*, or ladle, and a *wok chan*, or spatula. (You can use a slotted spoon or whatever you find convenient.) For right-handed cooks, the ladle is held in the left hand and the spatula in the right. The stirring motion is similar to the motion used when tossing a salad—a constant circular lifting and dropping of the ingredients.

Pao, the Chinese word for explosion, is another form of quick stir-frying. The heat is turned to the highest setting; therefore the process must be short and sharp, usually lasting no more than 1 minute, often less. The food is usually marinated, often cooked alone or combined with one or two other ingredients. In contrast, *Ch'ao* has as many as six foods fried together.

scramble frying: This is basically the same technique as quick stir-frying, but the ingredients are mixed with a true stirring or scrambling motion rather than the tossing motion used in quick stir-frying.

semi-deep-frying: Except in restaurants or food stalls, deep-frying in the Western sense is seldom seen in China. In the average household, food is semi-deep-fried in ⅔ to 1¼ cups of hot oil in a wok. A pair of bamboo chopsticks or a slotted spoon is used to turn the food over in the oil and push it up onto the sides of the wok. The advantage of the wok is that when the food is pushed onto its sloping sides, the oil will drain toward the center of the pan.

static-frying: There are two main categories of static-frying. *Chien:* larger ingredients may be used than in the various categories of quick stir-frying. Only limited stirring movements are used. *Tieh:* this differs from *Chien* in that usually the food is not turned over. Often the top side of the food is sprinkled with water, vinegar, broth, or a mixture of these. Thus the food produced will turn out soft on the top and crisp on the bottom. *Tieh* can also indicate foods which are cooked in large chunks or slices on both sides, and, after the cooking is completed, removed quickly from the pan and sliced into smaller pieces before serving.

stir-frying: See quick stir-frying.

wet-frying: This is called *Liu* and is a variation of quick stir-frying. Stirring is less vigorous and the stirring movements are aimed more at turning over the foods than mixing them. After the first phase of the frying, a sauce, consisting perhaps of cornstarch, broth, sugar, vinegar, and soy sauce, is introduced. The sauce is usually prepared in advance in a separate bowl and is added only 30 seconds to 1 minute before the cooking is complete. As soon as the sauce thickens the dish is served.

ginger root: a pungent aromatic herb with a coarse yellow skin, green inside, and white core. It varies from ¼ inch to 1 inch in diameter and 3 to 6 inches in length. Scrape the root before using. Thin slices (about ⅛ inch thick) are cut from the root as required. The unused portion should be wrapped in foil and will last for weeks. Store in a cool, dry place, in the refrigerator, or freeze without washing or scraping. Sliced fresh green ginger is available in 4½-oz. cans.

ginger water: prepared by placing 1 tablespoon chopped fresh ginger root in a pan with ⅓ cup water. Simmer over low heat for 3 minutes, strain, and use as required.

Hoisin, or Haisein, sauce (red vegetable sauce): thick

and viscous, brownish-red in color, with a pungent sweet spiciness about it, this sauce is made from soy beans, garlic, chili, sugar, and vinegar. It is used primarily in cooking, especially with shellfish, spareribs, pork, duck, chicken, and vegetables. It may be kept in a tightly sealed jar in the refrigerator for several months. If not available commercially, a substitute sauce may be prepared in the following manner:

3 tbs. soy sauce
1 tb. catsup or tomato paste
½ tsp. tabasco sauce
1 tb. sherry
1 tb. finely chopped onion
½ tsp. finely chopped ginger
½ tsp. finely chopped garlic
1 tb. salad oil

Blend ingredients together and heat over low flame until volume is reduced to half.

Kweichow salt-and-sour pickle: can be used with either meat or fish dishes, and in small quantities with other vegetable dishes.

Makes about 3¾ cups
3 cabbage hearts
6 cloves garlic
3 tsps. salt
3 tbs. dry sherry
3 tbs. salt
3 tbs. chili powder
2 tsps. sugar
2½ cups sweet sherry
Preheat the oven to 300.

Chop the cabbage hearts into ½-inch pieces. Crush the garlic and mix with the chopped cabbage hearts. Place in a casserole. Cover and cook in the preheated oven for 30 minutes. Remove from the oven and let cool for 2 hours. Sprinkle with the 3 tsps. salt. Pour the dry sherry over the mixture and mix well. Cover the casserole again and let the contents stand for 3 days at room temperature. After 3 days, mix in the 3 tbs. salt, chili powder, sugar, and sweet sherry. Pour the mixture into a sterilized airtight jar and seal. Let the mixture stand for 50 days.

For a simplified version, simmer ⅔ lb. spring greens and 2 cloves crushed garlic in 1 pint water (with 1 tb. salt) for 1 hour. Drain throughly. Sprinkle with 1 tsp. sugar and 2 tsps. chili powder. Cover with vinegar and let stand for at least 48 hours.

kumquats: small citrus fruits; kumquat plants are often grown as decorative miniature potted trees. Kumquats are usually preserved in a syrup and do not require refrigeration.

leechee, or litchi: a fruit with a thin brittle shell enclosing a sweet, jellylike pulp and a single seed. It is white and resembles a grape in texture. Sold fresh in summer, it is also available canned in a light syrup or dried. Unused fruit may be placed in its own syrup in a tightly sealed jar and refrigerated. Large sweet grapes with skins and seeds removed may be used as a substitute.

leeks: *See* scallion.

lotus leaves (water lily leaves): the leaves of the lotus plant, they come in large sheets, often more than 18 inches across. In Chinese cooking they are frequently used to wrap various foods and flavoring ingredients together before steaming them. The food thus absorbs the flavor of the leaf. A large cabbage leaf may be used as a substitute.

lotus root (water lily root): a reddish-brown tuberous stem similar in texture to a potato but better tasting and less woody. Soak for 20 minutes in hot water, rinse, then peel before using. As a substitute, use a raw or lightly boiled potato, or a turnip, lightly boiled to remove some of its flavor. These must not be overcooked and should retain their crunchy texture.

lotus seeds (water lily seeds): ovals about ½ inch long. They have a delicate flavor. To prepare, pour hot water over them and let stand for 5 minutes. Remove and discard the dark-brown husk and the small germ portion of the seed, which has a very bitter taste. Rinse in fresh water. Place in a pan, cover with water, and boil for 10 to 15 minutes. Drain and use as required. Blanched almonds may be substituted.

marinade: a pickling liquid consisting of wine or vinegar mixed with oil, spices, and herbs.

marinate: to place food (generally meat) in a marinade to absorb or release flavor, or to make the food more tender.

master broth (soy herbal sauce): a dark, aromatic sauce used to cook raw ingredients such as hard-boiled eggs, whole chicken, duck, or pork, kidney, or chicken livers. It eliminates unacceptable flavors and is used extensively to add a savory flavor.

Makes 7½ cups
3 bay leaves
3 sprigs parsley
1 sprig thyme
1 tsp. five-spice powder
7½ cups water
⅔ cup soy sauce
2 cups dry sherry
2 tsps. salt
½ cup brown sugar
2 tsps. monosodium glutamate
¼ tsp. pepper
2 tbs. dried tangerine (or orange) peel

Make a bouquet garni with the bay leaves, parsley, and thyme. Place it and all the other ingredients in a

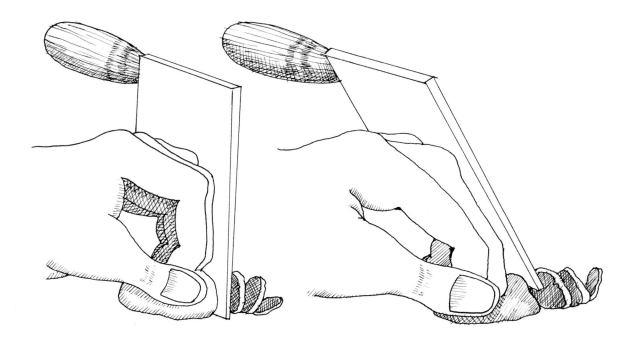

large earthenware pot (protected from the heat by an asbestos mat) and simmer for 1 hour. The broth is then ready and may be used repeatedly. It will keep indefinitely in the refrigerator. Each time it is used, the liquid is enriched further. It should be strained occasionally, and every third time it is used a fresh bouquet garni should be added, and then removed before refrigerating.

For a simplified version, boil 1 chicken bouillon cube, 6 tbs. soy sauce, 1½ tbs. brown sugar, 6 tbs. sherry, 2 bouquets garnis, (each consisting of 2 or 3 parsley sprigs, a bay leaf, and ¼ tsp. dried thyme tied in a square of washed cheesecloth), and 1 medium onion (chopped) in 1½ pints of water for 20 minutes.

monosodium glutamate: a white, powdery chemical that, when added in very small quantities, enhances or accentuates the taste of foods. When increasing quantities of a recipe, the amount of the monosodium glutamate should remain unaltered. Chicken bouillon cubes often contain a proportion of monosodium glutamate and may be used as a substitute. One cube equals 1 teaspoon monosodium glutamate.

noodles: *See* Chinese noodles.

oyster sauce: thick grayish-brown concentrate of oysters, soy sauce, and brine, it is used as a flavoring agent with meat, poultry, and seafood. It does not require refrigeration. If unavailable commercially, the following preparation may be substituted: Place the meat of 6–8 oysters, 6–8 tbs. soy sauce, and 2 tbs. dry sherry in a saucepan and simmer for 10 minutes or until the volume is reduced by one-third. Blend or mash until smooth.

pickled Szechwan cabbage: *See* cabbages.
plum sauce: a thick amber-red condiment made from plums, apricots, sugar, chili, and vinegar. It is generally used with roast duck, pork, and spareribs. It is only occasionally used in cooking. It is available in jars and cans. Plum sauce may be made at home using the following recipe:

12 dark plums
½ cup water
¼ cup soy jam
1 tb. sugar

Peel the plums, remove the pits, and cut into quarters. Place in a saucepan with the water and simmer, uncovered, over low heat until very soft. Add the soy jam and the sugar. Stir until sugar is dissolved and mixture is well blended.

red bean-curd cheese: *See* bean-curd cheese.
red cooking: stewing in soy sauce. Another method is first deep-frying, then braising in stock. Either way, the predominant seasoning is soy sauce.

rice flour: the flour derived from milling rice.

rock sugar, brown (rock candy): large grains or lumps of crystallized sugar; ordinary brown sugar may be substituted.

scallion: a member of the onion family. The Chinese generally use both the white and green parts of the scallion, cut into segments as required. The flavor is extracted by sautéeing in oil or fat.

sea cucumber: a species of jellyfish, it resembles a small, wrinkled cucumber. In China it is usually dried, gray-black, and 4 to 10 inches long. Before using, scrub and soak for 24 hours in warm water, changing the water several times. Clean carefully, removing the internal organs, then rinse in fresh water. When soaked, it becomes a gelatinous mass with some fairly hard parts. Sea cucumber is usually cooked with poultry, meat, or chicken broth. It is considered a delicacy and is eaten more for its texture than its taste, which is subtle to the point of being nonexistent. However, it enhances the flavor of the other foods cooked with it.

As a substitute: Soak beef or pork tripe in the refrigerator in several changes of salted water, with chopped ginger root added. After 2 or 3 days, cook in stock to cover in a 300° oven for 3 hours. Slice into strips 2 inches long by 1 inch wide.

secondary broth: a stock made from bones, frequently used in Chinese cooking. Place chicken bones, fresh pork bones, and smoked pork bones, in the ratio of 2:2:1, in a large saucepan. Cover with water 3 times the depth of the bones and simmer for 4 hours, skimming hourly.

For a simplified version, add 1 chicken bouillon cube to 1½ pints hot water. Stir until the cube is dissolved.

sesame jam (sesame paste): made from ground sesame seeds, it tastes and looks like peanut butter. It may be called *tahina* and is widely available. Sesame jam will keep for months if placed in a tightly covered jar and refrigerated. An adequate substitution is 6–8 tsps. peanut butter combined with 1 tsp. sesame oil.

sesame oil: made from toasted sesame seeds, it is similar to corn oil, with a strong, nutty taste and fragrance. Sesame oil is used sparingly as a flavoring agent (usually less than a teaspoon at a time).

sesame paste: *See* sesame jam.

soy jam (soy paste, soy bean paste): thick, viscous, almost black paste made from fermented soy beans. Soy jam, similar in flavor to soy sauce, is usually used where a thicker sauce is required—in the quick-frying of diced meat, for example. It may be bought in cans or jars. A substitute can be made by blending 1 tb. brown sugar, ½ tb. butter, and 5 or 6 finely mashed dates.

soy sauce: a sauce made from fermented soy beans,

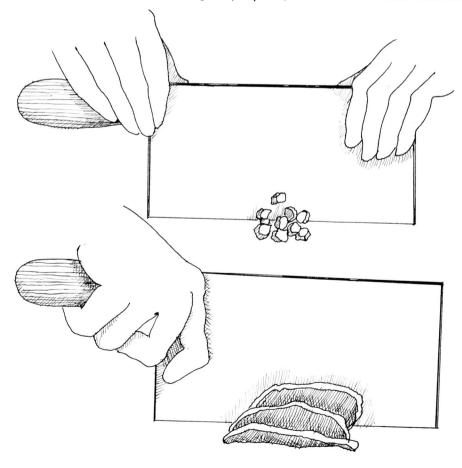

wheat, yeast, and salt. The sediment which forms is soy jam. Both the color and thickness of the sauce may vary from light to dark and thick to thin. For small quantities, 1 tsp. salt or 1 beef bouillon cube dissolved in a little hot water may be substituted for 2 tbs. soy sauce. For sweetened soy sauce, add 1 tb. sugar to 4 tbs. soy sauce.

light soy sauce: used where delicate flavor is desired without excessive color.

dark soy sauce: has caramel added; used where rich flavor and color are desired.

steaming: The steam produced from boiling rice is used to cook other foods by placing layers of steamers (basketwork trays called *jing loong*) on top of the container in which the rice is being cooked. These baskets are filled with vegetables, meats, or pastries that cook as the rice cooks and are usually ready at the same time. If a steamer is not available, you can make your own, using a large kettle or pan with a tight-fitting lid. Into this kettle place an ovenproof bowl at least one-third (but no more than one-half) the height of the kettle. Place an ovenproof plate or pie tin over the top of the bowl. Then place the food to be steamed, in its own container, on the plate. Fill the kettle with boiling water to *no more than one-third* the height of the ovenproof bowl. To achieve maximum results from your steamer it is important that this water level be maintained, and that the water, as it evaporates, is replaced with boiling water. Foods that cook in a short time may be left uncovered in the steamer. In any cooking over 30 minutes, however, the food container should be covered.

stir-frying: *See* frying: quick stir-frying.

superior broth: stock, which is essential in Chinese cooking. It is produced in quantity in China by a long process. A simplified recipe is given below. Canned chicken or beef bouillon may be substituted.

Makes 10 cups
1 2-lb. chicken or 2 lbs. chicken pieces
2 lbs. pork shoulder
2 lbs. pork bone
1 lb. smoked pork or ham bone
1 tb. chopped onion
1 tsp. chopped fresh ginger root
1 tb. soy sauce

Remove the breast meat and the 2 drumsticks from the chicken. Boil the remainder with the pork shoulder and bones in water to cover for 15 minutes. Meanwhile, finely chop the meat from the chicken breast and drumsticks, keeping the light and dark meat separate, and set aside.

Skim the broth. Lift out the chicken, pork, and bones. Place them in a bowl with 2½ pints cold water. Pour half of this water into the broth. The coolness coagulates the grease and impurities, making them easier to remove. Skim. Pour one-quarter of the broth into another bowl to cool. This cooling broth will be used as the bowl of cold water was used earlier. Return the chicken, pork, and bones to the broth. Simmer the mixture gently for 1 hour. It is important not to allow the broth to reach a full boil at any time, as this will create a cloudy broth. After 1 hour, remove the chicken, pork, and bones and place in the remaining cold water. Add the cooling broth to the pan, thus again coagulating more grease and impurities, which should once again be removed. This process is repeated 2 or 3 times until the broth becomes strong and pure.

In the final phase, add the onion, ginger root, and soy sauce to the broth. The chopped chicken meat is used as the final clarifier. The dark meat from the drumsticks is the first clarifier and the white meat is the second clarifier. In each case, the chopped chicken is simmered in the broth for about 10 minutes. Then the broth is strained through a sieve and the meat, onion, and ginger root discarded. The broth will keep for 3 to 4 days in the refrigerator. For making larger quantities, a duck may be added for every 2 chickens, but only chicken meat should be used for clarifying. For lighter broth, a frog and chicken combination is considered the best (in the proportion of 1 to 2).

Szechwan salted cabbage: *See* cabbages.

water chestnuts: a root vegetable, round and somewhat flat in shape, they have sweet, sugary juice and a crunchy texture. Available canned, water chestnuts are commonly mixed with ground meats to add crunchiness. They may be kept covered with water in a tightly sealed jar in the refrigerator for a week if the water is changed every few days. New potatoes, cooked for no more than 3 minutes, may be substituted for water chestnuts.

wine-sediment paste: a thick paste made from wine sediment and fermented rice. Wine-sediment paste is used in cooking meats, poultry, and seafood. It has the effect of strengthening the taste of food as well as diminishing pronounced fish flavor. An acceptable substitute may be made by blending together in an electric blender 1 tb. red bean-curd cheese, 1 large onion, finely chopped, 1 tsp. finely chopped ginger root, 2 tsps. finely chopped tangerine (or orange) peel, 2 tsps. brown sugar, 2 crushed garlic cloves, ¼ cup dry sherry, 1 tb. tomato paste, 1 tsp. fine rice flour, 1 tb. brandy (optional), and ¼ cup red wine. Reduce the volume of the mixture by one-third to one-half by simmering over low heat in a large shallow skillet. The resulting paste should be red and thick.

winter melon: pumpkin size, with light-green skin which is coated with white. The meat is white. A cucumber, young squash, or zucchini may be substituted.

wok: an iron or aluminum pan shaped like a cone with a rounded bottom. (Rings, or bases, are sold to adapt woks to range-top cooking.) The advantages to cooking with a wok are that food can be quickly and evenly cooked over high heat in little oil. Iron woks should be seasoned with oil and never scoured after use; eventually they turn black. A size of 12 or 14 inches is adequate for home use. *See also* frying.

wood-ears: a species of lichen. The type most often used in Chinese cooking is black in color and dried. Before using, soak for about an hour and clean in several changes of water. Like bamboo shoots, they are used more for their texture (crunchy and slippery) than for their taste, which is bland. The cloud-ear is white and shaped like a cloud, as its name indicates. There is also silver-ear fungus. This is sometimes used in sweetened soups. Button mushrooms may be used as a substitute.

Yunan ham: *See* Chinese ham.

China

Approximately one-third larger than the continental United States, China is primarily an agricultural country in that the majority of the people make their living from the soil. Very little of the land, however, is fit for agricultural development. China abounds in mountains, deserts, eroded land, and rough climate, and only about 11 percent of the land is capable of being cultivated.

The traditional cooking of this heavily populated country was born of necessity, dictated by economic hardship, hunger, and scarcity of livestock. To satisfy their nutritional needs and flavor-craving palates, the people of China had to approach the preparation of food with all the inventiveness at their command.

The Chinese not only "marry" a tremendous variety of ingredients, they also use the technique of *multistage* heating. Food may be steamed first, then quick-fried; or boiled first, simmered until almost dried, and quick-fried to a crescendo at the last minute; or deep-fried first, then quick-fried with other ingredients.

Flavoring, too, is a multiphase operation. Food may be marinated before cooking, after steaming, or between the first and second quick-fryings. The possible combinations in this cooking method are innumerable. When the food is cooked without the addition of spices, the diners usually choose from a wide range of table dips and mixes, both dry and liquid, to give piquancy to the simply cooked food. The dipping style of eating is an integral part of Chinese food preparation and presentation.

Because Chinese cooking has resisted being turned into a precise science, there are no specific rules in the matter of timing, quantities, flavorings, and heating. In many recipes, correction is possible up to the moment the dish is served. To talk to a Chinese chef about time and quantities is tantamount to talking to an artist about inches or the weight of paint used in a picture composition! Once you have experimented with a few Chinese dishes, you will find yourself developing a feeling for it, in terms of what quantities of which ingredients are roughly needed to serve how many people.

It would be a Herculean task to try to obtain an over-all picture of all the regional cooking of such a vast country, whose people are so provincially oriented. But how interesting it would be to be able to observe and sample the food in China's restaurants, compared to that of the so-called chop suey houses that have grown up in the West. (Chop suey, incidentally, has been described as something the Chinese know only as "an agreeable foreign dish.") The average people of China know only the food of their own kitchens. The competent housewife must be a flexible chef, prepared to feed as many as a half-dozen extra guests, should they happen to show up at meal-time. There are snack specialists and tea-houses, and roving round-the-clock street vendors, who sell "small eats" —food cooked on the spot. The Chinese, like the Americans, relish casual eating.

In this book, we describe the characteristic food and cooking of ten regions of China. It is hoped that the Western reader will enjoy and enrich his table with these culinary ideas from another land.

Whether a neophyte or one of those already indoctrinated in Chinese cooking, you will find your culinary adventure easier and more enjoyable if you first familiarize yourself with the contents of the Glossary. Then, having chosen a recipe that interests you, purchase and assemble from your own larder all the necessary ingredients—and cooking equipment. Here, now, are some helpful pointers:
• Check the Glossary for the specific *method* of cooking to be employed. The Chinese use various methods, each involving a certain technique and timing.
• Study the recipe so that you know which ingredients must be chopped, diced, sliced, or whatever—and place each prepared ingredient in a small bowl.
• Ready all the condiments, measured out or mixed as called for in the recipe.
• Have all the required utensils at hand. Once you start the actual cooking, there won't be time to start scrounging in drawers and cupboards for that spatula or ladle.
• Line up everything on a tray or board in the order in which it will be used in the cooking process. Some things may need to be cooked a bit longer than others, and would naturally go into the pot first.

Peking

All Chinese are sentimental about the ancient city of Peking, which they affectionately call *Ku Tu* (the Old Capital). The harmonious beauty of all of Peking is man-made, from the architectural majesty of its high walls and broad main streets to the incredible Imperial Palaces and their grounds laced with pools, gardens, and artificial hills. Ten thousand pagodas have been counted in and around Peking. "Serenity" is the first word that comes to mind; in fact, the city has been renamed Peiping, meaning "Northern Peace."

Peking cuisine has been described as the top table of classical Chinese culinary art and the metropolitan cooking of China. Yet, setting aside the Palace's Imperial Kitchen and the culinary contributions from other regions, Peking cooking has only a limited range of dishes. It cannot compare with the diversified and enormous repertoires of East China or the southern provinces.

Because of the abundance of sheep in Mongolia (Peking borders on its desert), one emphasis is on mutton and lamb. Another is on the locally bred ducks. The dish known as Peking Duck is, of course, world-famous. The Chinese usually follow this dish with a rich, sweet cabbage soup made from the duck's carcass.

The Yellow River supplies excellent fish, and the Gulf of Chihli provides large shrimp. River crabs are very popular, and some restaurants serve them to the exclusion of everything else.

The cuisine emphasizes the great white cabbage, which is used in so many ways that a table is considered incomplete without cabbage in some form. Many dishes are also prepared with carrots, radishes, spinach, greens, and (in the summer) tomatoes. Garlic, ginger, onions, shallots, and leeks are an integral part of the cooking here.

As in other northern regions, wheat flour, rather than rice, is the staple food of Peking. It is generously reflected in the cuisine in many forms: steamed bread and buns (made either plain or with a deliciously seasoned meat filling), hot wheatcakes that are eaten with everything, and steamed dumplings so solid that two helpings constitute a meal. Chinese crescents (*chiaotse*) are everyday fare to the Northern Chinese, just as pasta is to the Italian. This raviolilike food consists of a piece of dough filled with vegetables and lamb or pork; it is then boiled, or fried and steamed, or it is eaten boiled with soy sauce and vinegar. There are many varieties of noodles, and one of the favorite dishes is simply a big bowl of steaming noodles with tasty sauces stirred in.

The people of Peking are fond of barbecued meat and dishes cooked at the table. Much of the food is prepared with wine stock. A popular form of communal eating revolves around the *huoko*, a chafing dish containing hot sauces into which small pieces of raw meats and vegetables are dipped. Although the cuisine of the northern provinces and Peking is generally lighter and more subtly seasoned than its southern cousins (who don't find it very exciting), it includes various pungent, sweet-and-sour dishes for spicier palates.

Every autumn, clouds of dust are swept into the city by the dry winds, blanketing everything with a velvety layer of fine dust. Even this has been given a loving place in the Chinese culinary culture, with the delicious dessert known as Peking Dust—a puréed chestnut mixture topped with a mound of whipped cream.

The pinnacle of lavishness in Chinese cooking and eating was reached in those long-ago mandarin and inter-mandarin banquets, when important government officials and bureaucrats entertained each other. In a country with no captains of industry or cardinals and bishops to dilute the scene, these men—the country and provincial heads and emissaries from the court of Peking—were the only lords of the land. Often they were very learned and discriminating, and very fussy about their food. Inasmuch as they held the power of life and death in their hands, they had no problem in getting provisions of superb quality. In the matter of outdoing one another in banqueting, no holds were barred. The zenith was probably reached in the "Great All-China Manchu Banquet" (*Man Han Chuan Hsi*), which ran to three hundred courses.

In the Palace of the Forbidden City of Peking, the catering was done by a number of Imperial Kitchens, which included the Breakfast, Supper, Banquet, and Picnic Kitchens, as well as the Kitchen for Worship and the Grand Altar, and one for visiting mandarins. Altogether, they employed over a thousand chefs and cooks.

When considering Peking cuisine as a whole, one must take into account all the classical dishes handed down from the Imperial Kitchens, as well as all the metropolitan dishes. The range, then, is considerable, and comparable with that of any section of Chinese cooking.

Hot and Sour Soup

SUAN LA T'ANG

3 tbs. cornstarch
⅓ cup water
3 tbs. soy sauce
⅓ cup vinegar
½ tsp. black pepper
¼ cup bean curd (optional)
1 egg
2 dried Chinese mushrooms,
    soaked and drained
½ small chicken breast
1½ tsps. lard
3 tbs. chopped onion
3¾ cups beef bouillon
1 tsp. monosodium glutamate
    (optional)
1 tsp. sesame oil
½ tsp. salt

In Chinese homes, this soup is served throughout the meal, rather than as a first course.

Tomato and Beef Broth

HSI HUNG SHIH NIU JOU T'ANG

1 lb. stewing beef
4–6 large tomatoes (1 lb.)
6 cups water
1 tsp. salt
1 tsp. monosodium glutamate
    (optional)

Although chicken blood (solid form) and bean curd are usually included in the original recipe, they are dispensable. To be successful, the broth must be well seasoned before the hotness (pepper) and sourness (vinegar) are added.

Blend the cornstarch with the water. Add the soy sauce, vinegar, and pepper and mix them together. Cut the bean curd into ¼-inch squares. Crack the egg into a cup and beat well with a fork. Cut the mushrooms and chicken flesh into matchstick-thin strips.

Heat the lard in a large skillet. Add the onion and sauté for two minutes. Add the bouillon, then the bean curd, mushrooms, and chicken. Bring to a boil and simmer for 15 minutes. Add the cornstarch mixture and optional monosodium glutamate. Stir the soup until it begins to thicken. Keep the soup swirling in the skillet and add the beaten egg slowly, pouring it down the tines of a fork so that it separates into threads. Add the sesame oil and salt.

Give the soup an additional stir so that the "egg-flower" (as it is called in China) will mix evenly with the rich brown soup. Pour into a heated tureen and serve immediately.

The combination of meat, tomatoes, and prolonged cooking produces a highly tasty and satisfying soup.

Cut the beef into 1-inch cubes. Place in a saucepan with boiling water to cover and boil for 2 minutes. Drain. Cut the tomatoes into pieces. Place the tomatoes and beef in a heavy saucepan and pour in the measured water.

Bring the contents of the saucepan to a boil. Reduce the heat to low (preferably placing the pan on an asbestos mat) and simmer very gently for 3½ hours. Add the salt, optional monosodium glutamate, and pepper to taste 5 minutes before serving. Pour into a large heated tureen and serve.

Peking Duck

PEKING K'AO YA

1 duckling, about 4–6 lbs
3 tbs. sugar
1 tb. dry sherry
3 tbs. water
30 doilies
15 scallions or 1 cucumber

FOR GARLIC-VINEGAR DIP:
6 cloves garlic
½ cup vinegar

FOR MUSTARD-SOY SAUCE DIP:
1 tsp. dry mustard
3 tbs. soy sauce

FOR CHILI-SOY SAUCE DIP:
1 tb. chili sauce
¼ cup soy sauce

> To clean the duck, wash it thoroughly inside and out in cold running water, rub it inside and out with the juice and pulp of two quartered lemons, then rinse in cold water.
>
> For easy handling, securely tie a piece of strong cotton cord around the feet of the duck, leaving a tail of cord about 1 foot long. This will give you something to hold when you dip the duck in boiling water to scald it. The duck can be hung by this cord to dry overnight after scalding, and again to dry after being rubbed with sweetened water.

This world-famous dish owes its fascination not only to the way it is cooked but also to the way it is eaten—wrapped in a doily (pancake) with scallion or cucumber and daubed with sauces. The combination of duck, fresh, crunchy scallion, and piquant sauces is delicious and unusual. This is a simplified version of the "official" recipe, which is over fifteen thousand words long.

Clean the duckling thoroughly and lower it for a moment into a pan of boiling water to scald. Dry immediately with paper towels and hang by the feet to dry overnight in a cool, airy place.

Mix together the sugar, sherry, and water, adding a pinch of salt to help the sugar dissolve. Rub the outside of the duck with this sweetened water several hours before roasting. Hang to dry again. When dry, rub the duck a second time with the sweetened water.

Preheat the oven to 375.

Place the duck in the oven on a rack with a pan underneath to catch the drippings. Roast for 20 minutes; then lower the temperature to 300 for one hour. Finally, raise the temperature to 400 for 20 minutes. The duck should then be well cooked and the skin very crispy. While the duck is cooking, prepare the doilies according to the instructions given in the glossary, using double the quantities listed. Chop the scallions into segments 2 inches long. If using the cucumber, peel and cut into thin strips about 2 inches long.

For the garlic-vinegar dip, crush the cloves of garlic and mix them with the vinegar. For the mustard-soy sauce dip, combine the dry mustard with the soy sauce. For the chili-soy sauce dip, combine the chili sauce with the soy sauce. Plum sauce and Haisein sauce are also traditionally served with the dish.

Carving the duck is done at the dining table. At the first carving, only the skin is sliced off. Pieces of this are placed on a heated plate and passed around the table. Each diner opens a doily on his plate, dips 1 or 2 pieces of the skin in sauces of his choice (saucers of which are scattered over the table), and puts the skin on the doily. Finally, he places a piece of scallion or a strip of cucumber on his doily, folds over the lower end, and rolls up the doily. This is eaten with the fingers while the duck skin is still crackling and warm. Repeat the process until all the sliceable meat has been carved from the duck.

Deep-fried Laminated Pork

KUO T'IEH LI CHI

½ lb. pork tenderloin
½ tsp. salt
1 tb. soy sauce
1 tb. dry sherry
½ tsp. monosodium glutamate
  (optional)
1 tb. chopped scallion
1 tsp. chopped fresh ginger root
½ cup all-purpose flour
1 egg
3 tbs. water
¼ lb. fatback
2 tbs. cornstarch
vegetable oil for deep-frying
fresh parsley or chives

Tip-out Steamed Pork

K'OU JOU

2½ lbs. pork, arm roast or fresh
  Boston shoulder with skin
⅓ cup soy sauce
½ cup vegetable oil
⅔ cup secondary broth
1 tb. sugar
3 tbs. dry sherry
½ tsp. salt
1 tb. chopped fresh ginger root
3 tbs. chopped onion

This is one of the "laminated" dishes derived from the former Imperial Kitchen.

Cut the pork into ¼-inch slices and marinate in the salt, soy sauce, sherry, optional monosodium glutamate, scallions, and ginger for 30 minutes. Blend together the flour, egg, and half the water. Coat the pork with this batter. Cut the fatback into paper-thin slices 4 to 6 inches long. Place the coated pork between sheets of fatback to form a sandwich. Press together on a board. Add the cornstarch and the remaining water to the batter and coat the sandwiches. Deep-fry each in oil over low heat for 4 minutes. Turn the heat to high and continue to cook for 3 minutes, or until a deep golden color.

Chop each sandwich into 4 pieces with single strokes without slicing backward and forward. Arrange on a dish and garnish with chopped parsley or chives. Serve with a dip consisting of 2 parts salt to 1 part pepper.

Arranging meat in a bowl and tipping it out after cooking is a typical Chinese way of cooking and serving. In this case, steaming is the last process; the pork is first boiled and fried.

Place the whole piece of pork in a saucepan and cover with water. Bring to a boil and simmer for 15 minutes; then drain. Set aside 1 tablespoon of the soy sauce and roll the pork in the remainder until coated. Heat the oil in a skillet and brown the pork on all sides for 10 minutes. Drain, cool, and cut the pork into pieces 2 inches by 1 inch by ½ inch, cutting across the meat so the skin is attached.

Arrange the pieces of pork, skinside down, in the bottom of a bowl. Heat the 1 tablespoon of soy sauce, the broth, sugar, sherry, salt, ginger, and onion for 1 minute and pour it over the pork. Place the bowl in a steamer, cover, and steam for 1 hour.

To serve, turn the bowl over onto a dish and tip out the pork so the skin will be on top. Hence it is called "tip-out pork." Both the meat and the skin will then be quite tender and the gravy extremely tasty.

Sometimes in Chinese meals one is surprised at the tenderness and crispness of chicken which seems only to have been fried. This recipe gives the secret.

Rub the chicken and cavity with the salt and five-spice powder. Mix together the tangerine peel, onion, ginger, soy sauce, sugar, and sherry. Coat the chicken with this mixture inside and out and let it marinate for 8 hours. Remove the chicken from the marinade, put it into the top of a double boiler, cover, and steam gently for 3½ hours. Replenish the boiling water when necessary.

Heat the oil in a deep-fryer. Gently remove the hot chicken from the double boiler and drain in a wire basket for 1 minute. Hold the cover of the deep-fryer in one hand and with the other hand plunge the wire basket with the chicken into the hot oil. Cover the fryer for 2 minutes; then remove the cover for 3 minutes. Remove the chicken, drain, and place on a plate. Surround it with the quartered tomatoes and shredded cabbage.

Aromatic and Crisp Chicken

KUEI FEI CHI

1 3-lb. chicken
1½ tsps. salt
½ tsp. five-spice powder
1 tb. chopped dried tangerine
   peel
1 tb. chopped onion
1 tsp. chopped fresh ginger root
3 tbs. soy sauce
1½ tsps. sugar
1 tb. dry sherry
vegetable oil for deep-frying
2 tomatoes, quartered
¼ lb. cabbage heart

The people of Peking seem to like sour and sweet, with the emphasis on sour. This dish is a kind of Chinese sauerkraut, although it is a little more piquant. Because of its sourness, this is a good dish to serve with rich food. Because of its spiciness, it is also a good dish to serve with plain rice. Hence, it is a popular dish with both the rich and the poor.

Remove and discard the coarse outer leaves of the cabbage. Cut off and discard the bottom and cut the heart and inner leaves diagonally into 1½-inch-long strips. In a bowl, mix the cornstarch, water, vinegar, soy sauce, sugar, and sherry.

Heat the oil in a large skillet and sauté the chili peppers for 1 minute. Discard the peppers. Add the cabbage and stir-fry over high heat for 3 minutes. Add the salt, broth, and optional monosodium glutamate. Continue to stir-fry for 5 more minutes over medium heat. Add the cornstarch mixture. Mix well with the cabbage. Stir-fry gently for 1 minute. Serve in a heated dish.

Sour and Sweet Cabbage

TS'U LIU PAI TS'AI

2–3 lb. Chinese cabbage
1 tb. cornstarch
1 tb. water
¼ cup vinegar
1 tb. soy sauce
1 tb. sugar
1 tb. dry sherry
¼ cup vegetable oil
2 dried chili peppers
1 tsp. salt
¼ cup secondary broth
½ tsp. monosodium glutamate
   (optional)

Quick-fried Pork

CHIANG PAO JOU TING

1 lb. pork tenderloin
1 egg
1 tb. cornstarch
vegetable oil for deep-frying
3 tbs. vegetable oil
3 tbs. soy jam
2 tsps. sugar
2 tsps. dry sherry
2 tsps. ginger water

> For cooking, the Chinese use extra-long chopsticks. You can substitute a wooden spoon or whatever you find convenient.

The people of Peking dice meat into cubes and then cook it quickly with a few ingredients. The process is a highly efficient way of making meat extremely tasty in a short time.

Cover the pork with cold water and refrigerate for 30 minutes. Drain and cut into ½-inch cubes. Beat the egg in a bowl and stir in the cubes of pork. Add the cornstarch and mix thoroughly. Heat the oil and deep-fry the meat cubes for 2 minutes (using chopsticks to keep the pieces of meat apart). Drain and set aside.

Heat the 3 tablespoons oil in a skillet over medium heat. When hot, stir in the soy jam. Then add the sugar, sherry, and ginger water. Turn the heat to high and stir for 15 seconds. Add the meat cubes and scramble-fry for 30 to 40 seconds. Serve immediately on a heated plate.

Quick-fried Sliced Fish

CHUA CH'AO YÜ P'IEN

½ lb. fish fillets (sea bass, rock cod, haddock, or sole)
6 tbs. cornstarch
2½ cups vegetable oil for semideep-frying

FOR THE SAUCE:
1 tb. soy sauce
1 tb. sugar
1 tb. dry sherry
2 tsps. vinegar
½ tsp. monosodium glutamate (optional)
2 tsps. cornstarch
1 tb. water
2 tbs. lard
1 tb. chopped scallion
1 tsp. chopped fresh ginger root

Many former Imperial chefs, now in their eighties, are employed by Peking restaurants. This recipe is from the famous ex-Imperial chef Wang Yü Shan. It is a fairly simple and tasty way to prepare many different kinds of fish, and is one of Wang Yü Shan's favorite recipes.

Slice the fillets into strips, 1½ inches by ¾ inch by ¼ inch. Dredge in the cornstarch. Semideep-fry the pieces of fish in the vegetable oil in a large skillet, adding each piece of fish separately (so they can be handled gently and do not stick to each other). The frying should be gentle, over low to medium heat, and the fish should be removed after 2 minutes. Drain, and set aside while preparing the sauce.

Mix together in a bowl the soy sauce, sugar, sherry, vinegar, monosodium glutamate, and cornstarch blended with the water. Stir and mix well. Discard the oil in the skillet and add the lard. When hot, add the scallion and ginger and fry for 30 seconds. Pour in the mixture from the bowl and stir until the sauce thickens. Return the slices of fish to the skillet. Turn them over in the sauce a few times and then transfer to a heated dish. Serve immediately.

Yang Kuei Fei was the most famous royal concubine of the Tang Dynasty, hence the dish is also known as Kuei Fei chicken. This recipe is the Chinese version of coq au vin. *It is a very warming dish and, therefore, popular in the winter. It is usually served halfway through a 10- or 12-course banquet, immediately after the quick-fried dishes.*

Rub the chicken inside and out with 2 teaspoons of the sherry and half the soy sauce. Chop the scallions into segments 1-inch long.

Deep-fry the chicken in hot oil for 7 to 8 minutes, or until it is just beginning to turn golden. Remove it, drain, and plunge into a pan of boiling water to remove most of the oil remaining on its surface. Place the chicken in a large ovenproof dish or casserole and pour the bouillon on top. Deep-fry the scallions for 1 minute and add them to the casserole, along with the remaining sherry, soy sauce, optional monosodium glutamate, and salt. Cover and simmer over low heat for 2 hours. Add the wine and simmer for another 20 to 30 minutes. Both the chicken and the soup it has been cooked in should be served from a large heated tureen.

Royal Concubine Chicken

HSIANG SU YU CHI

1 3-lb. chicken
3 tbs. dry sherry
3 tbs. soy sauce
6 scallions
vegetable oil for deep-frying
7½ cups chicken bouillon
1 tsp. monosodium glutamate (optional)
½ tsp. salt
¼ cup red wine

The chicken should be tender enough to take apart with a pair of chopsticks. The soup is marvelously tasty.

Lamb Hot Pot

SUAN YONG JOU

4–5 lbs. lamb (about ½ lb. per
    person)
1 lb. Chinese celery cabbage
¼ lb. spinach
3¾ cups hot secondary broth
3¾ cups hot chicken bouillon
¼ lb. transparent noodles

FOR THE DIPS:
soy sauce
sesame oil
sesame paste
vinegar
chili sauce
tomato sauce
shrimp sauce
prepared mustard
sugar and ground garlic
coriander
scallion

Any container that can withstand direct heat and hold at
least 7½ cups of boiling liquid
along with the other ingredients can be used for this dish.
An alcohol burner, canned heat,
or a small electric stove can be
used as a source of heat. (An
electric hot plate will not provide sufficient heat, and charcoal stoves should not be used
indoors because of the danger of
carbon monoxide poisoning.)
The contents must be kept at a
rolling boil, and the hot pot
should be very steady so it will
not tip over while the cooking is
in progress. Fondue forks can be
used instead of chopsticks, but
never put a metal fork that has
been in the hot pot to your lips.
A nasty burn can result. Give
each diner one fork for cooking
and another for eating.

*Cooking thinly sliced lamb in a hot pot at the table dates
from the nineteenth century, and has become one of the
features of Peking. The attraction of this dish lies in the simplicity of materials, the freshness resulting from instant
cooking, and the effect of the piquant dips.*

Cut the lamb into paper-thin slices 7 inches by 2½ inches
and place on small plates, about 15 pieces on each. Shred
the cabbage and discard the spinach stems.

Put both the hot secondary broth and chicken bouillon into
a hot pot or a large casserole that can withstand direct heat
and place over high heat at the table. As soon as the broth
starts to boil, add about one-quarter of the prepared vegetables and the noodles. Within 1 to 2 minutes the liquid
will reboil. At that moment each diner immerses his own
slices of meat in the boiling liquid with chopsticks. Meanwhile, the diner mixes his dip in an empty bowl in front of
him. The dip may be a mixture of some or all of the ingredients listed for the dips. The diner may even have 2 or more
bowls of different dips for his own use.

The meat should be cooked for about 1 minute in the boiling broth. It should then be dipped in the sauce or sauces
before eating. The remaining vegetables and noodles are
added to the hot pot as the meal progresses.

By Chinese standards, this dish appears rather sweet, but the last Empress of China was well known for her sweet tooth and her taste must have influenced the methods used by her chefs.

Remove and discard the skin and halve the kidneys. Slash each half with crisscross cuts ¼-inch deep. Cut each half into pieces 1½ inches by ½ inch. Dredge in the cornstarch. Heat the oil in a large skillet and semideep fry the meat for 2 minutes over low heat, adding each piece separately. Remove, drain, and set aside.

In a bowl mix the soy sauce, sugar, sherry, vinegar, optional monosodium glutamate, and cornstarch blended with the water. Discard the oil in the skillet and add the lard. Heat, then add the shallot and ginger and sauté for 30 seconds. Add the soy-sauce mixture and stir until the sauce thickens. Return the meat to the skillet and coat in the sauce. Serve immediately on a heated dish.

Quick-fried Pork Kidneys

CHUA CH'AO YAO HUA

½ lb. pork kidneys
¼ cup cornstarch
vegetable oil for deep-frying

FOR THE SAUCE:
1 tb. soy sauce
1½ tsps. sugar
1 tb. dry sherry
2 tsps. vinegar
½ tsp. monosodium glutamate (optional)
2 tsps. cornstarch
3 tbs. water
2 tbs. lard
1 tb. chopped onion or shallot
1 tsp. chopped fresh ginger root

Toward the end of spring, after a rainless autumn and winter, the North China Plain is dry and dust storms often blow in from the Inner Mongolian desert. But the "Peking dust" here is made from chestnuts.

Make a crisscross cut on the flat side of each chestnut. Plunge them into boiling water and simmer for 40 minutes. Drain, remove the shells and skins, and grind the chestnuts finely. Blend in the salt and half the sugar. Whip the cream and fold in the remaining sugar (and a little vanilla extract to taste, if desired).

Form a mound of "dust" in a bowl for each diner. Top with the whipped cream and garnish with candied fruit.

Peking Dust

LI TZU FEN

2 lbs. chestnuts
½ tsp. salt
⅔ cup sugar
1¼ cups heavy cream
vanilla extract (optional)
6–8 pieces candied fruit

Honeyed Apples

PA SSU P'ING KUO

6 medium apples (2 lbs.), peeled
   and cored
1 egg, beaten
3 tbs. all-purpose flour
vegetable oil for deep-frying
⅓ cup sugar
3 tbs. vegetable oil
¼ cup water
¼ cup corn syrup

> Sesame seeds sprinkled in the hot syrup before the apple pieces are added make an interesting variation to this delightful recipe. Use the seeds sparingly, for their flavor can overpower the delicate bouquet of the apples.

The Chinese do not have many desserts in their culinary repertoire, but this unusual one is popular. The contrast in textures of the crisp toffee and soft apple is one of the charms of this dish.

Cut the apples into pieces 1½ inches long by ½ inch wide. Dip the apple pieces in the egg and dredge with flour. Heat the oil in a deep pot and deep-fry the apples for 2½ minutes; then drain. Heat the sugar and 3 tablespoons oil in an ovenproof dish. When the sugar has melted, add the water, followed by the corn syrup. Continue to stir gently over the heat until the liquid has become golden. Add the apple pieces to the hot syrup, turning the pieces over so they are well coated, and bring to the table in the cooking dish.

Each diner should be provided with a bowl of ice water. Using his chopsticks, he draws a piece of apple from the cooking dish and plunges it into the water. The coating syrup instantly cools into a brittle hardness. After the dipping, the apple should be placed in a saucer to cool for a few moments before eating. In the process of dipping, the apple should not be left for any length of time in the water or it will become soggy.

Ice Mountain Fruit Salad

TS'UAN PING WAN

1 lb. apples
1 lb. pears
1 lb. peaches
1 honeydew melon
1 lb. cherries
3–4 cups strawberries (1 qt.)
1 lb. grapes
½ lb. water chestnuts
1 small pineapple
crushed ice

Cold and sweet, this dish appears in Peking toward early summer, usually as an appetizer. Sliced fresh lotus roots, fresh water chestnuts, and peaches are often used. Strawberries, pineapples, and other seasonal fruits can be added.

Peel and quarter the apples, pears, and peaches. Place them in ice water to prevent discoloration while preparing the other fruits. Halve the melon, remove the seeds, and cut the flesh into pieces about the same size as the other fruits. Rinse and pit the cherries and hull the strawberries. Peel and halve the grapes and remove the seeds. Slice the water chestnuts. Peel and slice the pineapple, removing the woody center core.

Make a bed of crushed ice on a large serving plate. Arrange the pieces of fruit on top in an artistic pattern, interspersing the fruits with larger chunks of ice. Alternatively, a raised mound of ice may be piled in the middle of the large serving plate to give the effect of a miniature ice mountain. Decorate the ice mountain with the fruit.

Szechwan

Szechwan has the largest population of any single province of China. Historically, the area was practically unknown until the latter part of the Han Dynasty, which ruled from about 200 B.C. to A.D. 200. By the time of the "Three Kingdoms" (A.D. 211–265), it was already referred to in the literature of the day as "Heaven's own mansion, where stretches of fertile fields roll away by the thousand miles."

Szechwan is very well endowed, producing quantities of rice and bamboo, which thrive in the clammy weather, and an abundance of wheat, corn, and sweet potatoes. Practically the entire gamut of the fruits that are so popular in China are grown in this region, and it is especially renowned for its tangerines. The salt mines of Szechwan are extensive. Above all, of course, the province is best known to the world at large for the panda, which lives in the bamboo forests of its western region.

Szechwan's large grain crops enable it to raise plentiful numbers of poultry and pigs. The ham here is quite superior. A nationally popular way of cooking pork is to boil it, then fry it; or to fry it, then steam it. This "double-cooked" method is alleged to have been conceived in Szechwan. The preponderance of pork and chicken in the diet of the region has led to imaginative use of spices, sauces, and relishes to lend variety to the cuisine. The dish known as "Strange Flavor Chicken" derives its name from the unusual flavor combination of its ingredients.

Since almost all fertile and arable lands are cultivated, there is not much grazing land. Consequently, this is not sheep country, and lamb is not eaten to the degree that it is in the North. However, there are quite a number of beef dishes among the native Szechwan recipes—supposedly because the haulage in the salt mines is done by oxen or steers, and some of the cattle bred for this purpose are used for food.

Even though the province is situated so far inland and landlocked, there are numerous rivers, ponds, and tributaries that supply freshwater fish, duck, and even shrimp. The fact that there isn't as much seafood in Szechwan as there is meat and poultry inspired the imaginative cooks of the region to concoct a specialty called "Mock Fish," a dish made of meat (pork, beef, or veal) with a sauce that reproduces the taste of fish.

In summer, Szechwan's climate is very hot and, as in many tropical countries, the people there like their food spicy and peppery hot. *Fagara*, an extremely hot and strongly flavored red pepper, is used in many dishes, but it is quite different from the ordinary pepper Westerners know. Those who are unfamiliar with this fiery spice are advised to treat it with respect. It has a delayed reaction: at first it seems to have no taste, but suddenly it burns the mouth with unbelieveable ferocity.

The pepper is intended as a stimulant to the taste buds, to "wake up" the palate and make it more sensitive to a simultaneous variety of flavors. The people of this province prefer multiflavored dishes. Sour, hot, sweet, and salty—all are combined in the Hot and Sour Soup, a famous regional specialty.

The salt produced in the area is used extensively in the cuisine, and perhaps with more skill and effect than elsewhere. As a by-product of salt, Szechwan also produces an exceptional range of pickles, which are frequently used in cooking fresh food for added piquancy.

There is naturally a very wide range of vegetables, plants, and fungi — as well as a sizable range of medicinal herbs—in this fertile and semi-tropical region. From the Chungking area comes a great variety of high-quality mushrooms. The city of Chungking, the biggest port in the province, clings to a crag two hundred feet high between the Yangtze and the Chia-ling Rivers. The fertile green mountains behind the town are full of springs, rivers, and brooks, spilling waterfalls and spreading mist down along the hillsides. The area is ablaze with tropical flowers and sweet-smelling gardenias, mimosa, cedars, and cypresses; lemon and orange and wild banana trees abound.

Dumplings are another specialty of the province—sesame dumplings, or those stuffed with pork and cabbage.

The quick stir-frying method of cooking, so popular in almost every other part of China, is not the predominant style of cooking in Szechwan kitchens. Steaming, simmering, and smoking are more often used.

Locally grown tea—a powerful brick variety—is well-adapted to the strong palates of the province. Brick tea is so called because of the technique (in ancient times as well as today) of compressing the loose tea, leaves, and stems into solid brick shapes. To make a cup of tea, a piece of the brick is simply cut off and boiled.

On the whole, the diet and dishes of Szechwan's cuisine, more than that of any other province, seem to embody the range and balance of Chinese cooking.

Hot Chicken in Peanuts

SUI MI CHI TING

3 large chicken breasts
1 tb. cornstarch
1 egg
½ cup shelled peanuts
2 scallions
1 tb. water
1½ tsps. sugar
2 tsps. vinegar
1½ tsps. soy sauce
½ tsp. salt
vegetable oil for deep-frying
4 tsps. dried chili peppers
2 tbs. lard

Fish-broth Hot Pot

CHÜ HUA YÜ KENG KUO

1½ cups transparent pea-starch
  noodles
vegetable oil for deep-frying
½ cup shelled peanuts
½ small Chinese celery cabbage
  heart
¼ lb. spinach
1 cup bean sprouts
1 cup watercress
2 scallions
3 slices fresh ginger root
few sprigs parsley
½ lb. fish fillet (sole, carp, cod,
  or halibut)
1 large chicken breast
¼ lb. chicken livers
¼ lb. pork liver
fish bones, head, and tail
6 cups chicken bouillon
1½ tsps. salt
1 large chrysanthemum blossom
1 tb. lard
½ tsp. monosodium glutamate
  (optional)

Many Peking officials were appointed to Szechwan and they exercised a considerable influence in culinary matters. This recipe is for a Peking-style dish cooked with local Szechwan materials like peanuts and hot seasonings.

Dice the chicken. In a bowl mix half the cornstarch and the egg. Stir in the chicken. Grind the peanuts coarsely. Chop the scallions into ½-inch segments and combine with the remainder of the cornstarch blended with the water, sugar, vinegar, soy sauce, and salt. Deep-fry the diced chicken in the hot oil for 30 seconds. Drain and set aside. Remove and discard the seeds and chop the chili peppers. Heat the lard in a skillet and sauté the chili peppers for 30 seconds. Add the chicken and stir-fry for 10 seconds. Pour in the scallion mixture and continue to stir-fry for 20 seconds. Sprinkle in the peanuts. After a few stirs, pour onto a serving dish.

There are many versions of hot pot recipes throughout China, but this fishbroth version is the Szechwan favorite. Although the chrysanthemum is the most common flower used in this form of hot pot, other flowers such as peach blossom may also be used. Accordingly, the dish is sometimes called "chrysanthemum hot pot" or "peach blossom hot pot."

Deep-fry the noodles in the hot oil just until they puff up. Then drain. Deep-fry the peanuts quickly until brown and crisp. Arrange them in two plates and place on the dining table. Wash and trim the cabbage, spinach, bean sprouts, and watercress and place them neatly on 4 other plates. Cut the scallions into ½-inch lengths and place on a dish with the ginger and the parsley. Clean the fish and cut into very thin slices, 2 inches by 1½ inches. Slice the chicken, chicken livers, and pork liver into similar-sized pieces.

Prepare a fish broth by boiling the fish bones, head, and tail for 5 minutes in the chicken bouillon, along with the scallions, ginger, parsley, and salt. Strain and reserve the broth.

Loosen and remove the petals of the chrysanthemum blossom and arrange on a small dish, imitating as nearly as possible the shape of the original bloom.

Heat the reserved broth and pour it into the hot pot, which is then placed over high heat in the center of the table in front of the diners. When the broth boils, drop in all the chrysanthemum petals. Add the fish, chicken, and livers. When the contents come to a boil again, add the noodles, peanuts, cabbage, and watercress, followed by the spinach and bean sprouts. Add pepper to taste, the lard, and optional monosodium glutamate. Allow to reboil for 25 seconds. Pick the various ingredients out of the pot with a pair of bamboo chopsticks or a slotted spoon and place in the diner's rice bowl.

The items from the pot may also be dipped in various mixes and dips such as salt-pepper, soy sauce-vinegar, or Haisein sauce, which are placed conveniently on the table. Not all the food needs to be cooked in the pot at the same time. Different quantities can be put in at various stages.

At a Chinese meal, each diner will have his own bowl of rice into which are put the foods from the hot pot. Whether or not it is served in individual bowls, there should be copious amounts of rice at the table.

Traditionally the chrysanthemum hot pot is fired with methylated spirit and is quite similar to a Swiss fondue set.

Quite often toward the end of many courses all the suitable leftovers are put into the pot for one last boil. This can result in an extremely interesting final course that is especially satisfying on a chilly autumn or winter evening.

Vegetarian Noodles

T'UNG CHING HSIANG SU-MIEN

¼ cup sesame paste
1 tb. sesame oil
3 tbs. wine vinegar
1 tsp. monosodium glutamate
  (optional)
1 tb. sugar
3 tbs. soy sauce
1 tsp. chili sauce
1 lb. Chinese noodles (or
  spaghetti)
3 tbs. finely chopped scallion
  stems
1 tb. finely chopped garlic

Originally, this was a popular dish of the masses, who often prepared it to entertain their friends and relatives on special occasions. It was also served from mobile stalls which were carried on shoulder poles, with a charcoal cooker and wash-bowl at one end, and the bowls, utensils, chopsticks, and spoons at the other.

Mix together the sesame paste, sesame oil, vinegar, optional monosodium glutamate, sugar, soy sauce, chili sauce, and pepper to taste. Divide among the diners.

Boil the noodles or spaghetti for 10 to 15 minutes. Drain, and while steaming hot, place a portion on top of the mixture given to each of the diners. Sprinkle the noodles with the scallion stems and garlic. Each diner uses his own chopsticks to toss and mix the noodles or spaghetti.

Szechwan salted cabbage gives a spicy flavor to the bamboo and chicken. It is ideal to accompany rice and meat dishes.

Remove and discard the outer layers of the bamboo shoots and reserve the softer hearts. Slice these lengthwise into strips, ¼-inch thick by ½-inch wide, and then cut into segments 1½ inches by 2 inches in length. Finely chop the pickled cabbage.

Heat the lard in a skillet. When hot, pour in the bamboo shoots and stir-fry for 1 minute. Remove the bamboo shoots and set aside. Sauté the pickled cabbage in the lard remaining in the skillet for 1 minute over medium heat. Return the bamboo shoots to the skillet and stir-fry together with the cabbage for 1 minute.

Pour in the chicken broth, salt, sherry, and optional monosodium glutamate. Simmer for 3 minutes. Add the cornstarch blended with the water. Continue to stir-fry gently. Add the chicken fat in small pieces before serving on a heated flat dish.

Fried Bamboo Shoots with Pickled Cabbage

YEN PAI T'SAI TUNG SUN

6 cups bamboo shoots
⅓ cup pickled Szechwan
    cabbage
2 tbs. lard
⅓ cup chicken broth
1 tsp. salt
3 tbs. dry sherry
1 tsp. monosodium glutamate
    (optional)
1½ tsps. cornstarch
2 tbs. water
1 tb. chicken fat

Quick-fried Ribbon of Duck

CHIANG PAO YA SSU

¾ lb. cooked or smoked duck
3 stalks celery
1 small leek
1 red sweet pepper
2 tsps. dried chili peppers
2 cloves garlic
¼ cup lard
1 tb. fermented black beans,
    soaked for 1 hour
1½ tsps. sugar
1 tb. soy sauce
1 tb. vinegar

This is a dish which carries a highly savory "punch." In all these quick-fried dishes, heat is supposed to carry and propel, in itself, a flavor of its own.

Slice the duck into matchstick-thin strips. Trim the celery and leek and cut into similar-sized strips. Remove and discard the seeds from the red sweet pepper. Cut into thin strips. Crush the garlic. Heat the lard in a skillet. Sauté the chili peppers in it for 1 minute to flavor the oil. Remove and discard the peppers. Add the celery, leek, garlic, red sweet pepper, and black beans. Stir-fry over high heat for 1 minute. Add the duck, sugar, and soy sauce. Continue to stir-fry for 1 minute. Finally, add the vinegar and stir-fry quickly for 10 seconds before serving.

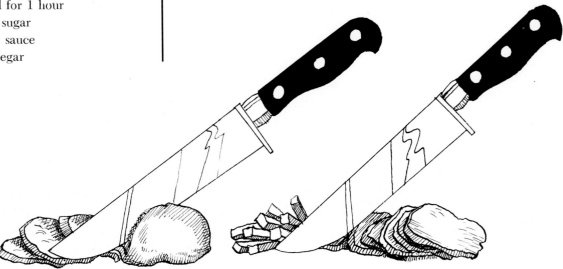

Steamed Pork with Pickled Cabbage

SHAO PAI

1½ lb. pork, fresh picnic
    shoulder or loin roast
vegetable oil for deep-frying
4½ tsps. sweet sherry
1 tb. soy sauce
1½ cups pickled Szechwan
    cabbage

Double-cooked pork is usually boiled first and fried afterwards. In this case it is deep-fried first and steamed afterwards, with other ingredients and seasonings added between the cooking processes.

Deep-fry the pork in hot oil for 10 minutes over medium heat. Drain, cool, and cut into slices, 2 inches by 1 inch, each piece containing both lean and fat. Arrange the pieces on a plate and add the sherry, soy sauce, and pepper to taste. Marinate for 10 minutes. Arrange the pork in neat layers in a large ovenproof bowl. Chop the cabbage and place over the pork. Cover and steam for 40 minutes. Serve on a heated plate with rice.

Double-cooked Pork

HUI KUO JOU

2 lbs. Boston butt or pork loin roast
1 small leek
1 tb. fermented black beans, soaked for 1 hour
1 tb. lard
1½ tsps. sugar
1 tb. soy sauce
1 tsp. chili sauce
2 tsps. plum or Haisein sauce

Double-cooked pork is said to have been first invented in Szechwan, although it is now popular throughout China. The green and red-brown color combination is quite attractive. This recipe comes from the Fei Yung Dining Rooms, in Chengtu the capital of Szechwan.

Boil the pork in water to cover for 20 minutes. Drain and cool for 30 minutes. Remove the skin and cut the pork into 1-inch-by-1½-inch slices. Each slice should have both lean and fat. Trim the leek so that there are equal parts of green and white. Cut into 1¼-inch-long segments. Mash the fermented beans into a paste.

Heat the lard in a skillet. Then add the pork and cook for 2 minutes over low heat. Add the sugar, soy sauce, chili sauce, and plum or Haisein sauce, and turn the heat to high. After 20 seconds of quick stir-frying, add the leek and continue to stir-fry for 1½ minutes. Transfer to a heated dish and serve immediately.

The multiplicity of flavors explains the name chosen for this dish. It is a great favorite in Szechwan and is gaining popularity throughout China.

Cook the drumsticks in boiling water to cover for 5 minutes; then simmer gently for 15 minutes. Drain and cool for 10 minutes. Remove the bone from the drumsticks and slice the flesh diagonally into 4 pieces.

Stir-fry the sesame seeds gently in a dry pan over very low heat until they are just turning golden and beginning to crackle. Place 1 tablespoon of the seeds in a dry bowl and pound the remaining 2 tablespoons to a powder in a mortar, adding the sesame oil to make a paste. Mix this paste with the soy sauce, sugar, vinegar, chili sauce, and pepper. Chop the white part of the scallions (reserving the green parts for use in another dish) and pile them in the center of a heated serving dish. Arrange the pieces of chicken around the edge by overlapping them, skinside out. Pour the sesame paste mixture evenly over the chicken and sprinkle the crispy, dry sesame seeds on top before serving.

Strange-flavor Chicken

KUAI-WEI CHI K'UAI

6–8 chicken drumsticks (about 1½ lbs.)
3 tbs. sesame seeds
1½ tsps. sesame oil
2 tbs. soy sauce
2 tsps. sugar
1 tb. vinegar
1 tsp. chili sauce
¼ tsp. black pepper
8 scallions

45

Salt-buried Chicken

YEN KUO CHI
1 2-lb. chicken
1 tb. soy sauce
6 scallions
4 tsps. chopped fresh ginger root
1 tsp. salt
3 tbs. cherry brandy
6 lbs. coarse (Kosher) salt

FOR THE DIP:
3 tbs. chopped scallions
2 tsps. chopped fresh ginger root
1 tsp. salt
⅓ cup secondary broth
2 tsps. salad oil

There are several recipes for salt-buried chicken. This one comes from the Pearl Dragon restaurant in Chengtu.

Dip the chicken in boiling water for a moment then pull and stretch it. Dip again and dry thoroughly. Rub the outside with the soy sauce and hang up to dry for 3 hours.

Wash the scallions and crush them with the side of a knife, so that they are slightly bruised. Put the ginger and scallions in a bowl and add the 1 teaspoon salt and the cherry brandy. Mix. When the chicken is dry, stuff it with this mixture. Heat the coarse salt in a large cast-iron pot. When quite hot, make a hole in the middle and bury the chicken. Cover the pot. Place it over low heat for 10 minutes. Remove from the heat and let stand for 10 minutes. Repeat this process twice more for a total of 1 hour. Alternatively, the pot can be placed in a preheated 325° oven for 1¼ hours. Remove the chicken from the salt and chop into pieces about 1¼ inches by ¾ inch. Discard the stuffing.

Arrange the chicken on a heated plate in a spread-eagle pattern. Serve with saucers of dip made by boiling the dip ingredients together for a few seconds.

Salty, sweet, sour, and hot all at the same time, this method of frying was brought to Szechwan from Peking.

Remove and discard the core and cut each kidney in half. Slash with crisscross cuts ¼ inch apart and two-thirds through the kidney. Cut into pieces, 1 inch by ¾ inch. Blend half of the cornstarch with 1 tablespoon of water, the sherry, and salt. Thoroughly coat the kidney pieces in this mixture. In a separate bowl, mix the sugar, vinegar, soy sauce, optional monosodium glutamate, and broth. Set aside. Cut the scallions and the leek into ½-inch pieces. Remove and discard the seeds from the chili pepper.

Heat the oil in a skillet until very hot. Add the kidney, spreading the pieces evenly; sauté for 15 seconds, and then drain. Discard all but 1 tablespoon of oil. In the same skillet, sauté the chili pepper for 1 minute and discard. Crush the garlic, then stir-fry the scallions, leek, garlic, ginger, and chili powder for 20 seconds. Add the kidney pieces and stir-fry for 10 seconds. Then gradually add the vinegar mixture and stir-fry the kidney gently for another 15 seconds. Add pepper to taste and serve immediately.

Hot-fried Kidneys

KUNG-PO YAO KUAI

¾ lb. pork kidneys
2 tbs. cornstarch
2 tbs. dry sherry
½ tsp. salt
1 tb. sugar
1 tb. vinegar
1 tb. soy sauce
½ tsp. monosodium glutamate
  (optional)
3 tbs. superior broth
3 scallions
1 dried chili pepper
1 small leek
⅓ cup vegetable oil
2 cloves garlic
3 slices fresh ginger root
¼ tsp. chili powder

Hot-braised Sliced Beef

SUI CHU NIU JOU

1 lb. beef tenderloin
1 egg
¼ cup cornstarch
1 tsp. salt
4 tsps. dried chili peppers
1 small green or red sweet
  pepper
⅓ cup vegetable oil
1 tb. fermented black beans,
  soaked for 1 hour
½ cup bamboo shoots
3 scallions
1 tb. chopped onion
1 tb. chopped fresh ginger root
1 tb. sliced leek
¼ tsp. black pepper
1 tb. dry sherry
2 tbs. dry white wine
⅔ cup superior broth
1 tsp. monosodium glutamate
  (optional)

If you have difficulty slicing meat very thinly, try putting it in the freezer for half an hour. The slightly frozen meat will be much easier to cut into the thin slices so often called for in Chinese cooking.

It is the usual process in Chinese cooking for quick-frying to be followed by a period of braise-simmering, when a little broth is added to the food. This recipe is a typical example of this method.

Cut the beef into thin slices, 1½ inches by 1 inch. Break the egg into a bowl. Add the cornstarch and salt and blend to a smooth batter. Add the beef and, using your fingers, coat the meat evenly with the batter.

Remove and discard the seeds from the chili and sweet pepper. Slice the sweet pepper into strips. Stir-fry the chili and sweet pepper in half the oil for 1½ minutes and set aside. Mash the fermented beans. Cut the bamboo shoots and scallions into 1½-inch segments.

Heat the remaining oil in a large skillet. Add the mashed beans, bamboo shoots, scallions, onion, ginger, leek, and pepper; stir-fry slowly over medium heat for 2 minutes. Add the sherry and wine, and after 10 seconds add the broth and optional monosodium glutamate. Turn the heat to high. When the contents reboil, add the coated beef. After 30 seconds, transfer to a deep serving dish. Meanwhile, reheat the chili and sweet pepper and pour them, together with the oil, over the beef.

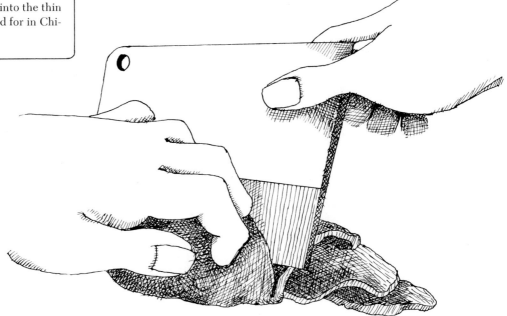

Shantung and Hopei

The great Yellow River, on its way to the sea, once flowed south of the province of Shantung, but a century ago, it changed its course northward by several hundred miles. The center of the province is a mountainous ridge that becomes a peninsula in the North China Sea.

The lower regions of the Yellow River were the cradle of Chinese civilization. The philosophers Confucius and Mencius were born and lived here, as did Lao-tse, founder of the Taoist school of philosophy.

The climate here is favorable to the growing and cultivating of bountiful crops. Although every part of China can be described as "chicken country," Shantung seems to be more so than any other. It is also a great cotton- and peanut-growing area, and a prolific producer of such fruits as pears, apples, grapes, melons, and peaches—the peaches so juicy that it is impossible to confuse them with those of any other region.

The "cabbage habit" of the Chinese is very much in evidence here. There are, of course, many varieties of this vegetable, the tastiest and most highly prized being the great white cabbage from the flatlands of Shantung. *Bok choy* ("white cabbage"), which has white celerylike stalks about a foot long, with large green leaves, finds its way into many marvelous dishes of the region. Another distinctive variety of Chinese celery cabbage is the crimson-colored *Tai an*, also very popular in North China.

Shantung cooking tends to be sweeter and spicier than that of the South, and it contains more fat. Sweet-and-sour seasoning was conceived here, originally for sliced carp. The Yellow River carp is treasured as a delicacy of the region, and any leftovers are used in sweet-and-sour soup.

Foods marinated in wine are typical of the cuisine. The emphasis in cooking methods is more on steaming, simmering, grilling, and deep-frying than on the quick stir-fry method. The provincial wine usually taken with meals is the popular Shantung rice wine.

Immediately north of Shantung is the province of Hopei, in which the capital of Peking is situtated. The seaboard here is flat and muddy, and offshore the large North China shrimp abound. Along with freshwater crab and mullet, they are a characteristic part of the regional diet.

Hopei is bordered in the west and north by the famous Great Wall of China, universally conceded to be the greatest building project in the world. This Eighth Wonder of the world, running mostly along the southern edge of the Mongolian plain, was built to protect China from northern barbarians. Ranging in height from fifteen to almost sixty feet, and twenty three feet thick, the awesome wall threads its way and climbs across China from one mountaintop to another, on and on for some fifteen hundred miles!

The Wall divides Hopei from Manchuria to the north and much of Inner Mongolia to the northwest. Just north of the Wall lies the arid Gobi Desert. The land south of the Wall, however, is quite lush, and conducive to the growing of wheat and corn. Grain, especially wheat for various kinds of bread, is more basic to the Northerner's diet than rice is. Steamed bread (mun-tao), a regional specialty, lends itself to a variety of accompanying tastes; for instance, it is eaten with such pungent vegetables as leeks, garlic, shallots, and onions, as well as a little meat, topped off with frequent and generous amounts of soy jam. Roasted potatoes are also a popular part of the robust fare.

The Chinese from this part of the country are particularly tall and heavy in build (six-footers are common). This often surprises Westerners, who are accustomed to the slight-statured Chinese from Hong Kong and Canton. A popular theory among the people of Shantung is that their impressive size—and their general immunity to germs—can be attributed to the fact that they eat their scallions raw.

The natives of this region prefer their chicken and meat (largely lamb) cooked simply: boiled, roasted, or barbecued. The taste of the food is heightened by dipping it into various types of mixes on the table: salt and pepper, chili and soy sauce, garlic and vinegar, plum sauce, sweetened soy jam, or Hoisin sauce.

The dish known as Peking Duck, made famous by the old chefs of the capital city in their desire to please the emperor, is enjoyed throughout the province. Much of the cuisine here is the so-called mandarin (meaning "Top Man of the Empire") style of cooking, a distinctly northern cuisine. In fact, the mandarin influence is seen in Chinese protocol for the seating of dinner guests: The guest of honor is always placed at the head of the table, so that he faces south (as did the top men of the empire in Peking, in the North).

All the cooking of North China, including Peking cuisine, derives much of its inspiration from these two provinces.

Red-cooked Pork with Chestnuts

PAN LI SHAO JOU

2 lbs. pork, fresh shoulder or loin roast
1 lb. chestnuts
3 tbs. vegetable oil
1 small onion, peeled and quartered
3 slices fresh ginger root
½ tsp. salt
3 tbs. soy sauce
2 cups secondary broth
1 tb. sugar
3 tbs. dry sherry

Chestnuts, like peanuts, are often used with meat in China. The process of red-cooking is like ordinary stewing, except for the use of soy sauce.

Wash the pork in hot water and cut into 1-inch cubes, each with both lean and fat. Slash the chestnuts and cook in boiling water for 20 to 25 minutes. Drain and remove the shells. Heat the oil in a heavy saucepan. Sauté the onion and ginger for 1 minute over medium heat. Add the pork and, raising the heat to high, stir-fry for 3 minutes. Add the salt and half the soy sauce. Stir-fry for 3 more minutes. Then pour in the broth. Bring to a boil, turn the heat to low, and simmer, covered, for 45 minutes, turning the meat over 3 or 4 times in the process.

Add the chestnuts, remaining soy sauce, sugar, and sherry. Continue with the slow-simmering for another 30 minutes, mixing the chestnuts with the meat and turning the mixture over gently 3 or 4 times. Serve with rice.

Dry-fried Shrimp

KAN SHAO HSIA JEN

2 lbs. cleaned, cooked shrimp
1 tsp. salt
1 tb. dry sherry
1 egg
1½ tsps. cornstarch
½ cup lard
1 tb. chopped scallion
1 tsp. chopped fresh ginger root
1½ tsps. light soy sauce

In this recipe the shrimp are cooked with as few other ingredients as possible, their taste heightened only by the heat and the flavor of scallion and ginger. Chef Yuan, whose recipe this is, does not use monosodium glutamate.

Carefully mix the shrimp in a bowl with the salt, half the sherry, the egg, and the cornstarch. Heat the lard in a large skillet until very hot. Add the shrimp and stir-fry quickly over high heat. After 45 seconds, pour off the fat, drain the shrimp, and set aside.

Add the remaining sherry, scallion, ginger, and soy sauce. Stir-fry quickly again over high heat for 20 seconds. Return the shrimp to the skillet and gently stir-fry for 20 seconds.

Serve in a heated dish and eat immediately.

Chicken Bundles

CH'AI PA CHI

1 3-lb. chicken or chicken pieces
¼ lb. cooked smoked ham
3 cups dried Chinese mushrooms, soaked and drained
¾ cup bamboo shoots
2 bunches scallions
3 tbs. dry sherry
1 tsp. salt
3 slices fresh ginger root
3 dried chili peppers
1 tb. soy sauce
⅔ cup chicken bouillon
1 tsp. monosodium glutamate (optional)

> Unless the recipe calls for it, the skin should be removed from chicken that is being cut into slices or strips.

This is a party dish which takes time to prepare. It has an interesting appearance, and the method of cooking is unique.

Cut the meat from the chicken and slice it into thin strips about 2½-inches long. Slice the ham, mushrooms, and bamboo shoots into similar-sized strips.

Reserve 3 scallions from one bunch. Remove the white bulbs from the remaining scallions and reserve for another dish. Soak the green stems in boiling water for a few seconds to soften. Then use pieces 4½ to 5 inches long to tie the sliced ingredients into small bundles, each containing some chicken, ham, mushroom, and bamboo strips. Use 2 or 3 stems to tie each bundle.

Arrange the bundles in a deep ovenproof casserole and sprinkle with half the sherry and half the salt. Chop the 3 whole scallions into ½-inch lengths. Lay the slices of ginger, chili peppers, and scallions over the bundles. Place in a steamer, cover, and steam for 1½ hours. Meanwhile, prepare the sauce by adding the soy sauce and remaining salt to the chicken bouillon. Bring to a boil and add the monosodium glutamate, remaining sherry, and pepper to taste. When the chicken bundles are ready, remove from the steamer and discard the loose ginger, chili peppers, and scallions. Pour the sauce over the bundles and serve.

Fried Potato Sticks

CH'AO TU TOU SSU

2 large potatoes
¼ cup vegetable oil
1 chili pepper, seeded and chopped
1 tb. chopped onion
1 tb. soy sauce
½ tsp. salt
1½ tsps. vinegar

When eaten at a meal in China, fried potatoes—like all other dishes—are meant to accompany rice and are treated like any other vegetable dish.

Peel the potatoes and cut lengthwise into thin slices. Place the slices on top of each other and cut into long, matchstick-thin sticks. Simmer the potatoes in boiling water for 2 minutes and drain.

Heat the oil in a skillet over high heat. Sauté the chili pepper for 15 seconds; then add the onion and sauté for an additional 30 seconds. Discard the chili pepper and onion. Add the potato sticks. Toss and turn them in the oil for 3 minutes. Add the soy sauce, salt, and vinegar. Continue to stir-fry, but more gently, for 1 minute and then drain on paper towels. Transfer to a flat, heated dish and serve.

The Tai An variety of Chinese celery cabbage is particularly well known in North China. The name of the dish comes from its crimson coral color.

Remove and discard the outer leaves of the cabbage and use only the heart. Cut each heart vertically into quarters and then again into pieces 1½ to 2 inches long. Slice the bamboo shoots and mushrooms into matchstick-thin strips. Remove the seeds from the sweet and chili peppers and slice in the same manner.

Plunge the cabbage into boiling water for 3 minutes. Drain and sprinkle with salt. Arrange on a large heated serving plate and keep warm.

Heat the sesame oil in a large skillet. Add the bamboo shoots, mushrooms, and prepared celery cabbage. Then stir-fry over high heat for 2 minutes. Add the soy sauce, sugar, vinegar, and tomato paste. Continue to stir-fry for 1 minute. Add the water and simmer for 3 minutes. Mix well and pour over the cabbage as a hot garnish.

❧

This recipe is unusual in that the chicken is marinated several times. It comes from chef Chen Hsi Hsing of Tsinan.

Prepare flavored sherry by soaking the scallion and dried chili pepper in the sherry overnight.

Clean and dry the chicken thoroughly. Rub with half the flavored sherry, half the soy sauce, and half the ginger water. Then allow the chicken to marinate along with the bay leaves for 30 minutes.

Heat the vegetable oil until very hot. Drain the chicken, remove the bay leaves from the marinade, and deep-fry the chicken in the hot oil for 5 minutes. Drain the chicken again and return to the marinade, adding the remaining flavored sherry, soy sauce, and ginger water to the marinade. Turn the chicken in the liquid until thoroughly coated; then return it to the hot oil and deep-fry a second time for another 5 to 6 minutes. Pour any remaining marinade into a large saucepan and heat gently. Drain the chicken and turn in the hot marinade for 5 to 6 seconds. Drain the chicken; then chop with a sharp knife into 1½-inch cubes, including the bones. Arrange the chopped chicken on a heated plate and serve with dips consisting of a pepper-salt mixture and a chili sauce-soy sauce mixture.

Coral Cabbage

SHAN HU PAI T'SAI

2 lbs. Chinese celery cabbage
¾ cup bamboo shoots
4–6 dried Chinese mushrooms, soaked and drained
1 large red sweet pepper
½ chili pepper
1 tsp. salt
3 tbs. sesame oil
1 tb. soy sauce
3 tbs. sugar
2 tbs. vinegar
1 tb. tomato paste
⅓ cup water

Deep-fried Marinated Chicken

YU LIN CHI

1 tb. chopped scallion
1 tsp. chopped dried chili pepper
¼ cup dry sherry
1 chicken, about 1½-2 lb.
¼ cup soy sauce
1 tb. ginger water
2 bay leaves
vegetable oil for deep-frying

A cleaver is best, but you can use a heavy-bladed knife for chopping the chicken. First, cut it apart at the joints. Then cut through the bones by striking the back of the knife with a mallet or hammer.

Braised Beef with Tomato

HSI HUNG SHIH HUANG
MEN NIU JOU

1½ lbs. boneless chuck
3¾ cups water
2–3 large tomatoes, peeled,
    seeded, and quartered
3 tbs. sugar
vegetable oil for deep-frying
2 cloves garlic, crushed
3 slices fresh ginger root
1 tb. chopped onion
1 tb. vegetable oil
3 tbs. soy sauce
2 tbs. dry sherry
⅔ cup superior broth
1 tb. cornstarch
½ tsp. monosodium glutamate
    (optional)
3 tbs. water
½ tsp. chili sauce

Pork of Original Preciousness

YÜAN PAO JOU

2½ lbs. fresh ham, butt half
1 tb. brown sugar
vegetable oil for deep-frying
1 tb. chopped onion
1 tb. chopped fresh ginger root
3 tbs. soy sauce
1 tb. dry sherry
1 tsp. red bean-curd cheese
3 tbs. superior broth
4 eggs

With broth and tomato this is an extremely tasty dish to accompany rice. The broth resulting from boiling the beef may be used separately to make an excellent soup.

Place the beef in a large saucepan with the water, bring to a boil, cover, and simmer gently for 2½ hours. When the beef is tender, drain and cut into 1-inch cubes. Place the tomatoes in a saucepan, add half the sugar, and simmer for 10 minutes until reduced to a puree. Pour this sweetened puree into a bowl.

Heat the oil in a pan and deep-fry the beef cubes for 1½ minutes. Drain the meat and set aside. Sauté the garlic, ginger, and onion in the 1 tablespoon of oil for 1 minute over medium heat. Add the remaining sugar, soy sauce, sherry, and superior broth. Add the beef and simmer for 5 minutes. Then add the tomato puree and simmer for 3 minutes. Blend the cornstarch and monosodium glutamate with the water. Add to the beef and stir over the heat. Sprinkle with the chili sauce and serve.

❧

There is a tradition in North China of cooking egg with meat as in this wholesome dish.

Simmer the pork in boiling water for 10 minutes. Remove from the pan and dry with a cloth. Rub the pork with half the brown sugar. Place it in a wire basket and deep-fry in hot oil for 10 minutes. Drain and cool.

Cut the meat with its skin still attached into slices ¼-inch thick. Discard the bone. Place the onion and ginger in the bottom of a deep ovenproof dish or casserole. Put the sliced pork in the dish, skinside down.

Mix half the soy sauce, the sherry, bean-curd cheese, broth and remaining brown sugar in a bowl. Pour the mixture over the pork. Place the dish in a steamer. Cover and steam for 1 hour.

Meanwhile, hard-boil the eggs, cool under cold running water, and shell them. Turn the eggs in the remaining soy sauce until they are thoroughly coated. Reheat the vegetable oil, deep-fry the eggs for 1 minute, and cut each egg in half. When the pork is ready, transfer it to a heated, deep dish. Arrange the eggs, yolkside up, on top of the pork.

Quickly prepared, tasty, and aromatic, this dish is served in every dining hall and cafe, as well as on the tables of elegant households—wherever the aromatic qualities of quick-fried garlic and onion are appreciated.

Cut the lamb against the grain into thin slices 2 inches by 1 inch. Blend the cornstarch with the water and mix with the meat. Cut the scallions diagonally into 2-inch segments (using the green parts as well as the white).

Heat half the oil in a large skillet over medium heat. When very hot, put in the meat mixture and spread it evenly over the bottom of the skillet. Stir-fry gently for 2 minutes. Remove the meat and set aside. Add the remaining oil to the skillet and sauté the scallions and garlic in it for 2 minutes. Return the lamb to the skillet and add the soy sauce, salt, sherry, and optional monosodium glutamate. Turn the heat to high and scramble-fry for 1 minute. Just before serving, add the sesame oil.

Scramble-fried Sliced Lamb

CHUNG PAO YANG JOU P'IEN

½ lb. leg of lamb
1 tb. cornstarch
1 tb. water
10 scallions
⅓ cup vegetable oil
3 cloves garlic, crushed
1 tb. soy sauce
½ tsp. salt
1 tb. dry sherry
½ tsp. monosodium glutamate (optional)
1 tsp. sesame oil

Sweet and Sour Carp

HUANG HO T'ANG T'SU LI YÜ

1 2-lb. carp
1½ tsps. salt
½ cup all-purpose flour
vegetable oil for deep-frying

FOR THE SAUCE:
1 tb. chopped scallion
2 tsps. chopped fresh ginger root
1 clove garlic, crushed
5 water chestnuts
2 bamboo shoots
½ cup wood-ears, soaked and
    drained
½ cup superior broth
1 tb. soy sauce
2 tbs. wine vinegar
3 tbs. sugar
3 tbs. dry sherry
2 tsps. cornstarch
3 tbs. vegetable oil

The Yellow River carp is a delicacy often mentioned in Chinese literature. The leftovers, including head and tail, are traditionally made into a sweet and sour soup.

Clean, scale, and wash the fish thoroughly. Slash it about ¼-inch deep on both sides at 1-inch intervals. Rub it inside and out with salt and let stand for 20 minutes. Then dredge the fish in the flour.

For the sauce, place the scallion, ginger, and garlic in a bowl. Thinly slice the water chestnuts and bamboo shoots and put them in a second bowl along with the wood-ears. Mix the cold broth, soy sauce, vinegar, sugar, sherry, and cornstarch in a third bowl.

Place the fish in a wire basket and deep-fry in hot oil for about 10 minutes, or until crisp and golden. Meanwhile, sauté the scallion, ginger, and garlic in the 3 tablespoons oil over high heat for 1 minute. Add the bamboo shoots, water chestnuts, and wood-ears; then stir-fry for 30 seconds. Add the broth mixture. Stir and let stand for 1 minute. Drain the fish, arrange on a heated serving dish, and immediately pour the sauce over it. Serve at once.

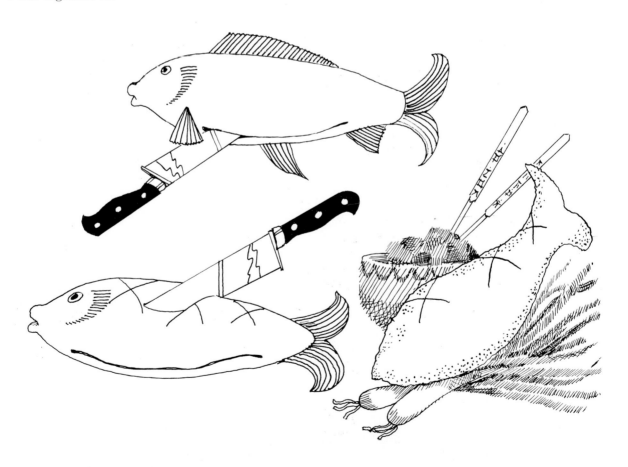

Scrambled Omelet

This is a scrambled omelet cooked with a small amount of shredded meat and one or two other ingredients. It is a popular dish with the people of northern China, and one very much suited for home cooking.

Beat the eggs in a bowl for a few seconds and add the salt. Shred the pork into matchstick-thin strips. Cut the mushrooms and scallions into thin strips or small pieces. Heat half the oil in a skillet and add the beaten eggs. Lower the heat and just before the eggs set completely, scramble slightly, remove from the skillet, and set aside.

Add the remaining oil to the skillet and place over high heat. Add the pork, mushrooms, and scallions. Sauté for 2 minutes; then add the soy sauce, broth, optional monosodium glutamate, and sugar. Cook for an additional 30 to 40 seconds. Add the scrambled egg, sherry, and sesame oil. Stir gently to mix all the ingredients and serve.

MU HSU JOU

4 eggs
½ tsp. salt
¼ lb. lean pork
8 dried Chinese mushrooms, soaked and drained
3 scallions
⅓ cup vegetable oil
1 tb. soy sauce
3 tbs. superior or secondary broth
½ tsp. monosodium glutamate (optional)
1 tsp. sugar
1 tb. dry sherry
1 tsp. sesame oil

Northwest China

China is the home of a fairly substantial Moslem population. By far the greatest concentration live in Sinkiang, the vast province to the extreme northwest, but there are Chinese Moslems scattered throughout the whole of the Great Northwest, which includes such provinces as Tsinghai, Ningshia, Kansu, Shenshi, and Inner Mongolia. Thus the Chinese Moslem cooking of the Northwest is one of the most widespread and best-established styles of cooking in China.

The cooking of the Northwest has also been influenced by the Mongols. During the dynasty (1279–1368) that ruled China after the invasion of the Mongols, Kublai Khan made his capital at Peking. He ruled the vast Mongolian empire (of which China, territorially, was considerably less than half) until his death, after which the invaders were finally driven out of China. The Mongols, lacking the culture of the Chinese, added little to the Chinese civilization except various foods and ways of preparing them. These the Chinese adapted to their less barbaric palates.

The whole of Northwest China is largely arid country, although there are many small streams that are fed by the mountain snows. Traditionally, the area has been so poor that its inhabitants, many of whom are nomads, existed barely above subsistence level. The Chinese here are more conservative and stolid than those of the South, perhaps because of the droughts and famines that have periodically torn the North. There is not enough rainfall, and the grazing lands are watered for the most part by streams and rivers.

To conserve fuel during the cold winters, the people burn a fire only to warm the air of the room being used. Rather than wastefully heat the whole house, they put on heavier clothes. The "fireplace" of the Northwest is simply a bed of brick or earth equipped with horizontal flues.

There are many points of similarity between Chinese Moslem and Israeli cooking. Both are widespread, and derived their original inspiration from the deserts. Pork, the principal meat of China, rarely appears in either (although the Chinese Moslems sometimes use it), and they are more inclined to use fish with scales than other forms of seafood.

Probably because of their nomadic desert background, the people of the Northwest have developed a cooking style that is the direct opposite of Cantonese cooking, which is full of sauces, delicacies, and elaborate dishes. The methods employed by the Chinese Moslems are basic: boiling (clear-simmering), barbecuing, and roasting. The Chinese words for this type of cooking are *Ching Tseng*—"clear and unadulterated."

Moslem cooking constitutes one of the three main inspirations of Peking cuisine and has a far greater influence on the capital's culinary repertoire than, say, Cantonese cooking. Such dishes as Mongolian hot pot (lamb), Mongolian barbecue (beef and lamb), and Peking duck (roasted by hanging in the oven) have come from the great central Asian background of Chinese Moslem cooking.

Mongolian hot pot is, as the name implies, a stewing pot of boiling water, into which thin pieces of beef or mutton are plunged. The enormous circular pot rests over a coal fire from which the smoke escapes through a chimney in the middle of the room.

The barbecue method of Mongolian cooking varies somewhat from the Western quick-grill style. A mouth-size piece of food (meat, fish, or fowl) is dipped into the barbecue sauce, grilled for a minute or so, and eaten at once. Again, according to old Chinese custom, the communal style of cooking and eating prevails; each person is his own cook and waiter.

The Mongolian style of cooking is well advanced in the technique of using earthen pots. In fact, there are some Chinese restaurants (such as Peking's Sa Kuo Chu, or "Home of the Earthen Pot") where the cooking is done only in earthen pots, which results in slow clear-simmering, rather than thick stewing. The aim is to subject the ingredients to prolonged undisturbed cooking, so that eventually they may be presented in a soup of dewlike purity.

When a form of cooking specializes in beef and lamb (a favorite of Northern cooks since the Mongolians first introduced it), it is bound to find itself limited unless it can make the best of all the bits and pieces of the animal. This is especially important in an infertile land where economy is paramount. Chinese Moslem cooking has, therefore, developed a considerable expertise in the use of tails, brains, feet, livers, and kidneys. Indeed, the use of these items is an essential part of the delicacy of this particular cuisine.

The strength and appeal of Chinese Moslem cooking is founded on its robust simplicity, as opposed to the general sophistication and complexity of Chinese cooking at large.

Long-simmered Beef

WEI NIU JOU

5 lbs. beef shank cross cuts
⅓ cup vegetable oil
3 tbs. sugar
¼ cup soy sauce
⅓ cup dry sherry
1 tb. dried tangerine (or orange) peel, soaked and drained
¼ cup finely chopped onion
2 tsps. chopped fresh ginger root

The beef in this dish is fried, boiled, and then simmered with flavoring until it is almost a meat jelly.

Trim the beef and cut into 1-inch cubes. Heat the oil in a skillet and stir-fry the beef for 4 to 5 minutes over medium heat. Drain the meat, place in a pan of boiling water, and boil for 3 minutes. Remove the meat and drain.

Place the beef in a heavy saucepan and barely cover with fresh cold water. Add the sugar, soy sauce, sherry, tangerine peel, onion, and ginger. Lower the heat as far as possible and simmer, tightly covered, for 4 hours. Stir the contents of the pan once each hour. Serve in a heated dish.

Braised Triple White

P'A SAN PAI

1 chicken breast
4–6 spears fresh asparagus
1 Chinese celery cabbage heart
3 tbs. chicken fat
1 small onion, sliced
3 slices fresh ginger root
⅔ cup superior broth
1 tb. dry sherry
1 tsp. salt
1 tb. cornstarch
1 tsp. monosodium glutamate (optional)
½ cup milk

In a multicourse Chinese dinner, a dish like this, which is light and pure in color, taste, and texture, introduces an essential variation in a long procession of dishes.

Cut the chicken breast into thin strips, 1½ inches by ¼ inch. Scrape the asparagus spears. Blanch both the asparagus spears and cabbage heart in boiling water for 1 minute. Then cut the asparagus and shred the cabbage into 1½- to 2-inch lengths. Place the chicken neatly on a plate along with the asparagus and cabbage.

Heat 2 tablespoons of the chicken fat in a skillet. Sauté the onion and ginger for 30 seconds. Add the broth and sherry. Bring to a boil, simmer for 1 minute, and then discard the onion and ginger. Add the chicken, asparagus, and cabbage to the skillet by lowering each separately into the boiling broth. Sprinkle with salt and cook for 3 minutes.

Blend the cornstarch and optional monosodium glutamate with the milk; then pour the mixture over the contents of the skillet. Return to a boil and stir gently until lightly thickened. Slip the remaining chicken fat into the side of the skillet and serve as soon as the fat has melted.

Quick-fried Tripe

LIANG CH'IH CHA PAO TU

2 lbs. precooked tripe
½ cup milk
2 tsps. salt
1 tb. vinegar
1 small clove garlic, crushed
1 egg white
1 tb. cornstarch
vegetable oil for deep-frying
¼ tsp. pepper
3 tbs. sesame oil

This recipe is served on two plates. Both dishes of tripe are snow-white, both are deep-fried, but one is then wet-fried. The contrast in textures makes a most interesting dish.

Wash the tripe, remove any membranes, and cut into pieces 2 inches by 1 inch. Divide into 2 portions. In one bowl mix together the milk, half the salt, the vinegar, and garlic. In another bowl, mix one portion of the tripe with the egg white and cornstarch until the tripe is well coated.

Heat the oil in a saucepan until very hot. Remove the pan from the heat and add the egg-coated tripe piece by piece. When all the pieces are in the pan, replace over the heat and deep-fry for 30 to 35 seconds. Remove the tripe and drain. The outside of the tripe should be almost crisp. Place on a heated dish, sprinkle with a mixture of the remaining salt and pepper, and keep warm. Reheat the oil. Add the second portion of tripe and deep-fry for 20 seconds. Drain the tripe and put in a pan with the prepared milk mixture. Stir-fry quickly for 10 seconds over high heat. Sprinkle with sesame oil. Serve both dishes of tripe at the same time.

Tartars' Barbecued Meat

HU JOU

5 lbs. fresh ham, shank half

FOR THE SAUCE:
1 tb. finely grated scallion
1 small clove garlic, crushed
3 tbs. soy sauce
1 tb. soy jam
½ tsp. dry mustard
2 tsps. sesame oil

This is a simple way to cook meat, as prepared at the Sa Kuo Chu Restaurant in Peking. The piquant sauce, used as a dip, gives added flavor.

Skewer the ham and rotate over a blazing open fire for 6 to 7 minutes, or until the outside of the pork begins to blister and burn. Alternatively, broil quickly for 8 to 10 minutes. Plunge the meat into cold water and let stand for 20 minutes. Remove from the water and brush off any burnt or discolored parts. Then place in a large saucepan with boiling water to cover and simmer for 1½ hours.

Make the sauce by combining the scallion, garlic, soy sauce, soy jam, mustard, and sesame oil. Drain and thickly slice the meat. Serve the ham on a heated dish with the sauce in a separate bowl.

According to backstairs culinary rumor, this dish originated in the great north in the kitchens and tables of the north-western bureaucrats—hence it is dainty compared with the more robust dishes of the region.

Cut the lamb into thin slices, 1½ inches by 1½ inches. Mix half the cornstarch with the soy jam and sugar. Coat the sliced lamb with this mixture. Mix the remaining cornstarch with the water in a second bowl. Add the ginger, soy sauce, vinegar, sherry, and sugar and blend to make a smooth mixture.

Heat the vegetable oil in a large skillet. When hot, add the lamb. Break up the slices and stir-fry quickly for not more than 15 seconds. Discard the oil and drain the lamb. Replace the skillet over the heat and return the lamb to it. Pour in the mixture from the second bowl and stir-fry quickly, this time for not more than 12 seconds. Sprinkle with sesame oil and serve.

Double-fried Honeyed Lamb

T'A SSU MI

¾ lb. lean fillet or leg of lamb
3 tbs. cornstarch
1 tb. soy jam
1 tsp. sugar
3 tbs. water
1 tb. chopped fresh ginger root
2 tbs. soy sauce
1 tb. vinegar
1 tb. dry sherry
4 tsps. sugar
⅔ cup vegetable oil
1 tb. sesame oil

These crisply fried beef fritters are dipped in salt and pepper before eating. Removing the skillet from the heat intermittently prevents the food from burning while achieving maximum crispness.

Cut the beef across the grain into thin slices, 1 inch by ½ inch. Place the slices in a bowl and add the onion, ginger, optional monosodium glutamate, sherry, and 2 teaspoons sesame oil. Mix well with the fingertips and set aside to marinate for 30 minutes. Break the egg into a bowl and add the flour and cornstarch. Blend and pour the mixture over the beef. Mix well. Heat the vegetable oil in a skillet. When hot, add the beef, piece by piece, spreading it out. Stir-fry gently over high heat for 2½ minutes. Remove the skillet from the heat for 1 minute, letting the beef simmer off the heat. Replace the skillet over high heat for 1 minute of gentle stir-frying. Once again remove the skillet from the heat for 1 minute. Repeat this process once more. After the third frying, drain the beef fritters and place them on a heated serving dish. Sprinkle with the remaining sesame oil. Mix the salt and pepper and use as a dip.

Beef Fritters

CHA NIU LI CHI

½ lb. beef tenderloin
1 tb. chopped onion
1 tb. chopped fresh ginger root
½ tsp. monosodium glutamate (optional)
1 tb. sweet sherry
1 tb. sesame oil
1 egg
¼ cup all-purpose flour
2 tbs. cornstarch
⅔ cup vegetable oil
1 tsp. salt
1 tsp. pepper

Bean Sprouts with Shredded Pork

TOU YA T'SAI CH'AO JOU SSU

¼ lb. lean pork
6 scallions
3 tbs. vegetable oil
1 tb. soy sauce
2 tsps. sugar
1 tb. dry sherry
1 clove garlic, crushed
1½ lbs. bean sprouts
1 tsp. salt

The dishes sold by the Municipal Caterers, of which this is a typical example, are seldom very elaborate. They are, therefore, easy to reproduce.

Cut the pork across the grain into matchstick-thin strips. Cut the scallions into 1½-inch segments. Heat the oil in a large skillet. Add the pork and sauté over high heat for 30 seconds. Add the soy sauce, sugar, and sherry. Stir-fry for 1 minute. Remove the meat and set aside to drain.

Add the garlic and scallions to the skillet and stir-fry for 15 seconds. Add the bean sprouts and sprinkle with the salt. Stir-fry and scramble for 1 minute, keeping the skillet over high heat. Replace the pork in the skillet. After 1 minute of stir-frying, transfer to a heated dish and serve.

This is a quick, easy, and appetizing way of preparing beef. The meat must be tender.

Slice the beef across the grain into thin slices, 1½ inches by ¾ inch. Place in a bowl and add half the soy sauce and the cornstarch. Mix together thoroughly. Cut the scallions into ½-inch segments.

Heat the oil in a skillet. Add the beef and gently stir-fry for 30 seconds. Drain and reserve the beef and the oil. Return the skillet to the heat and add 1 tablespoon of the reserved oil, the garlic, and the scallions. Stir-fry over high heat until the scallions are well browned. Add the beef, remaining soy sauce, sherry, water, and vinegar. Stir-fry quickly for 30 seconds and serve immediately.

Quick-fried Sliced Steak

HO CHIEN PAO JOU

¾ lb. beef tenderloin
3 tbs. soy sauce
1 tb. cornstarch
4 scallions
1¼ cups sesame oil for semideep-frying
1 clove garlic, crushed
1 tb. dry sherry
1 tb. water
1½ tsps. vinegar

67

East China

In Chinese history and literature, East China is referred to as "East-of-the-River," or sometimes "South-of-the-River." Geographically, it is really the south bank of the Yangtze River delta. Situated here is one of China's largest cities—Nanking, the old "Southern Capital" of China until the seat of government was moved north to Peking.

The other principal cities of the area are Soochow, Shanghai (China's largest city, with a population of over seven million), and Hangchow, all three cities enclosing a famous lake. The area immediately bordering the Yangtze consists of a mud flat delta which soon gives way to the fairly hilly, more picturesque areas to the south.

In contrast to the arid barrenness of the North, with its piercing winter wind, the climate and life South-of-the-River are much milder and easier. In the Yangtze River valley, even in its lower reaches, the winter is quite cold and the summer is swelteringly hot. Spring though is beautiful, and unmarred by the drought and dust storms of the north. And the autumn is one of long, windless sunshine, as it is everywhere else in China.

The men of letters here talked and wrote about flowers, reunions, brilliant conversations, boating banquets, and houseboats with concubines. All this created an atmosphere of good living and good eating. Yet life here is not overrefined, for this is also an area of many talents and tremendous enterprise.

The city of Nanking is surrounded by fertile rice fields and pleasing hills mantled in greenery and flowers; camellias are everywhere, and there is water wherever you look.

Shanghai, as it used to be, was a cross between Chicago and the Berlin of the Weimar Republic. It was a city brimful of sin, partly ruled by the Municipal Council of the International Concessions and the Japanese gunboats, and partly by the local gangsters and government officers, all trying to ride out the mounting tide of the Chinese Revolution.

Now Shanghai is principally an industrial center, destined to be one of the largest manufacturing cities in the world. Since it is a metropolitan city like Peking, its cuisine is a conglomerate of all the dishes of China. It enjoys an exceptionally wide range of seafood. Carp especially is plentiful, and is greatly relished in Shanghai.

The fish-filled rivers and the fertile land of this region produce such a copious yield that many of the foods are used rather extravagantly, sometimes just for flavoring: crab roe makes an interesting fat, shrimps suggest a nice seasoning, and the flavor of pork can lend just the right touch of sweetness to a dish. In Shanghai, a favorite pork dish is "The Salted Stews the Fresh," in which salted and fresh meat are simmered together.

Some of the best preserved foods come from Shanghai: salted fish and shrimps, shrimp eggs, dried bamboo shoots, mushrooms, and a myriad of other vegetables. Also very popular among the Chinese as an hors d'oeuvre is the lime-preserved hundred-year-old egg (best eaten when actually about one hundred days old).

A celebrated dish from this part of the coast is Bird's Nest Soup, an intricate but delicious soup made with an actual bird's nest cooked in chicken broth with minced chicken breasts. The nests are constructed by a certain type of swallow, which uses its own saliva in its home-building. The dried gelatinous substance, packaged and sold at Chinese grocery stores, is expensive. The soup is a real prestige dish, reserved for gourmet occasions.

Soochow, a mulberry-covered, silk-producing city, is reputed to produce the prettiest girls in China. They have light, smooth skins and extremely delicate bones and features. The streets of Soochow are very narrow and steep, in some cases hardly more than staircases. It is a city of gardens, with many ancient ones that are hypnotically beautiful.

The Grand Canal winds from Peking to Hangchow some thousand miles away in the North. The whole area is crisscrossed with streams, canals, and rivers which yield a wide variety of fish and shrimp.

Both Soochow and Hangchow have a reputation for exceptionally good "dot hearts" (*Tien-hsin*)—a "small eat" meal between meals, or, as the Chinese say, the "something to dot the heart." The "something" can also be a small thing eaten at a regular meal, such as a dough-thing that's been baked or boiled or fried. But it's never an actual dish, as such.

The city of Shao Hsing produces the best-known yellow rice in China, and the wine that is made from it is considered the best of all rice wines. Westerners usually need some time to get used to the idea of drinking their wine warm, as the Chinese drink it.

Wine is used a great deal in Chinese cooking, and we have included a recipe here for Shao Hsing (wine) soup. In China, of course, it's always the rice wines that are used for flavoring in cooking; for Westerners, the most satisfactory substitute is a dry sherry.

Ham in Honey Sauce

PING-T'ANG YÜAN T'I

1 3–4 lb. smoked ham, shank half
¼ cup lotus seeds
⅓ cup brown rock sugar
¼ cup boiling water
2 tbs. sugar
1 tb. honey
1 tb. cornstarch

This recipe comes from the Ta Hung Restaurant in Shanghai. The ham has a memorable flavor and is excellent for breaking the monotony of fried dishes in a multicourse dinner.

Soak the ham in water for several hours. Drain, place in a saucepan of cold water, bring to a boil, and simmer for 2 hours. Remove the ham, make a deep incision in the side, and remove the bone. Stuff the cavity with the lotus seeds and half the rock sugar. Place in a bowl, cover, and steam for 1 hour. Drain off the excess moisture and cut the ham into 15 pieces. Place on a dish with the lotus seeds on top. Sprinkle with the remaining rock sugar. Place the dish in a steamer, cover, and steam for an additional hour.

Drain the juices from the dish into a pan and add the boiling water, sugar, and honey. Bring to a boil. Thicken with the cornstarch blended with a little water and pour the sauce over the ham and lotus seeds before serving.

Squirrel Fish

SUNG SHU HÜ

1 3-lb. carp or bass
1 tsp. salt
¼ cup cornstarch
2 tbs. sugar
¼ cup vinegar
1 tb. soy sauce
6 tbs. chicken bouillon
¼ cup bamboo shoots
6–8 dried Chinese mushrooms, soaked and drained
vegetable oil for deep-frying
2 tbs. chopped onion
1½ tsps. chopped fresh ginger root
1 tb. lard

When scaling a fish, hold it with a piece of terry-cloth toweling to keep it from slipping.

This dish is called squirrel fish because as the sauce is poured over the hot fish it "chatters" like a squirrel.

Scale the fish and cut off the head. Slice open from head to tail and remove the bones. Clean thoroughly. Rub with salt, inside and out, and dredge thoroughly with half the cornstarch. Cut a dozen slashes on each side of the fish.

Mix the remaining cornstarch, sugar, vinegar, soy sauce, and chicken bouillon in a bowl. Cut the bamboo shoots into slices 1 inch by ½ inch. Cut the mushrooms into strips.

Place the fish in a wire basket. Lower it into very hot oil and deep-fry for 6 to 7 minutes. When the sizzling stops, reduce the heat. The fish will have curled. Allow the fish to cook very slowly for 2 more minutes. Turn up the heat and quickly deep-fry the fish for an additional 2 minutes. Drain and place on a heated oval dish.

Meanwhile, prepare the sauce by stir-frying the bamboo shoots, mushrooms, onion, and ginger in the lard. After 2 minutes, pour in the cornstarch mixture. Bring to a boil to thicken the sauce.

Bring the fish to the table immediately and pour the sauce over the fish at the table.

Soochow Melon Chicken

HSI KUA CHI

1 small chicken, about 1½ lbs.
5 cups water
¼ cup cooked smoked ham
⅓ cup bamboo shoots
8 dried Chinese mushrooms, soaked and drained
4 slices fresh ginger root
1½ tsps. salt
3 tbs. dry sherry
1 large honeydew melon
1 tsp. monosodium glutamate (optional)

The whole small chicken is steamed inside a hollowed-out melon—the melon lid is lifted off at the table to reveal the chicken inside.

Boil the chicken in the water for 2 minutes. Remove the chicken and rinse it in fresh water. Skim the broth. Thinly slice the ham and bamboo shoots, cut the mushrooms into strips, and marinate in 1½ cups of the broth with the ginger, salt, and sherry. Return the chicken to the remaining broth. Place in a steamer, cover, and steam for 1 hour.

Cut a lid off the melon and set aside. Carefully scoop out the melon, leaving the wall at least ½ inch thick. Reserve half the melon flesh for another dish.

Place the melon shell in a large bowl and fit the steamed chicken inside it, breast upward. Arrange the ham, bamboo shoots, and mushrooms on the chicken. Slip pieces of the melon flesh down the side around the chicken. Add the optional monosodium glutamate to the marinade and carefully pour this into the melon. Replace the lid of the melon and secure it with 3 toothpicks. Place the bowl in a steamer, cover, and steam for 20 minutes. Remove the bowl from the steamer and bring it to the table. Lift off the melon lid and serve the chicken from the melon shell.

Soft-fried Crabmeat

CH'AO HSIA FEN

1 lb. crabmeat
3 tbs. chopped onion
¼ cup dry sherry
1 tb. cornstarch
3 tbs. water
2 tbs. fatback
3 tbs. lard
1 tb. soy sauce
1½ tsps. sugar
⅓ cup chicken bouillon
2 tbs. ginger water

There is a local saying that "after crab nothing has any flavor," which gives an idea of how prized a delicacy crab is in this region.

Mix the crabmeat with half the onion and half the sherry. Blend the cornstarch with the water. Cut the fatback into small cubes. Heat 2 tablespoons of lard in a skillet. Add the remaining onion and fatback and sauté until golden. Add the crabmeat mixture and stir-fry very gently without breaking it into pieces. After 30 seconds add the remaining sherry, soy sauce, sugar, chicken bouillon, ginger water, and a pinch of salt. Mix gently and simmer for 3 minutes. Add the cornstarch mixture and remaining lard. When it boils, the dish is ready. The usual dips used in China for this dish are mixtures of chopped ginger root with vinegar, or chopped garlic with vinegar.

Here is a simple recipe that will appeal to a connoisseur. Since the total cooking time is less than 3 minutes, the fresh taste of the ingredients is preserved. The lard provides smoothness and the sherry liveliness. In Shanghai the locally caught river shrimp are used in this soup and they are not shelled before cooking. In the West, it is best to shell the shrimp first.

Cut the bamboo shoots into wedge-shaped pieces. Clean the watercress thoroughly and remove the stems. Cut the cucumber into the same sized pieces as the bamboo shoots.

Bring the broth to a boil in a saucepan. Add the bamboo shoots. After 1 minute, add the cucumber, followed by the watercress, shrimp, and salt. Lower the heat and simmer for 1 minute. Add the lard, the 3 tbs. of dry sherry, and optional monosodium glutamate. Pour into a large heated tureen and serve immediately.

Shad is one of the rare fish which does not need scaling. This is a delicious recipe from this area, which specializes in fish.

Remove the head and fins of the shad but not the scales, which are edible. Cut the fish in half lengthwise. Reserve half the fish for another dish. Clean and soak the remaining half in water for 1 hour.

Dry the fish and rub the scale side with half the soy sauce. Mix the remaining soy sauce, the bamboo shoots, sugar, sherry, salt, ginger, onion, mushrooms, and mushroom water (liquid in which the mushrooms were soaked) in a bowl and set aside.

Heat the lard in a skillet. Fry the fatback for 2 minutes. Spread the cubes around the skillet evenly and place the fish on top of them, scaleside down. Fry without stirring for 5 minutes. Turn the fish over and fry on the other side. After 1 minute, pour off the excess lard and add the soy-sauce mixture. Lower the heat and simmer until cooked, about 15 minutes.

Lift the fish out onto a plate. Turn the heat to high and add the cornstarch, blended with a little water, to the fish liquid. Bring to a boil and stir for 30 seconds until the sauce thickens. Then pour the sauce over the fish and serve.

Shao Hsing Soup

SHAO HSING T'ANG

2 bamboo shoots
½ bunch watercress
½ small cucumber
2½ cups superior broth
¼ lb. cooked, shelled shrimp
1½ tsps. salt
1 tb. lard
3 tbs. dry sherry
1 tsp. monosodium glutamate (optional)

Red-cooked Shad

HUNG SHAO SHIH YÜ

1 4–5 lb. shad
3 tbs. soy sauce
¼ cup bamboo shoots, sliced
1 tb. sugar
3 tbs. sherry
1 tsp. salt
1 tb. chopped fresh ginger root
1 tb. chopped onion
1 cup dried Chinese mushrooms, soaked in 1¼ cups water
3 tbs. lard
1 tb. fatback, cubed
1 tb. cornstarch

Use only half of a 4- to 5-pound shad rather than a 2- to 2½-pound one, because the smaller fish will be far too bony.

73

Spareribs and Water Chestnuts

KU CHIANG YÜ NI

1½ lbs. spareribs
12 water chestnuts
2 tbs. lard
2 tbs. chopped onion
1 tsp. chopped fresh ginger root
2 tbs. sugar
3 tbs. dry sherry
3 tbs. soy sauce
⅔ cup water
½ cup superior broth
1 tsp. monosodium glutamate
    (optional)
1 tb. cornstarch

Shrimp-topped Pork

FU YUNG JOU

1 lb. pork tenderloin
¼ lb. fatback
20 cooked shelled shrimp
sesame or vegetable oil for
    deep-frying
3 tbs. sesame oil
1 tb. finely chopped green or red
    sweet pepper
1 tb. dry sherry
2 tbs. soy sauce
3 tbs. wine-sediment paste
1 tsp. monosodium glutamate
    (optional)

Not elegant enough for a feast or banquet, this extremely tasty dish is essentially for home cooking.

Separate the spareribs and chop them into 1½-inch pieces. Cut the water chestnuts into quarters, if large, or halves, if small. Heat the lard in a skillet and fry the spareribs for 5 to 6 minutes, until they turn brown. Add the onion, ginger, sugar, half the sherry, half the soy sauce, and the water. Cover and simmer gently for 30 minutes.

By this time there should be about ¼- to ⅓-cup of liquid left in the pan. Turn the heat to high and bring the contents of the pan to a rolling boil. Add the water chestnuts and broth. Stir the contents gently with a wooden spoon.

When the liquid is reduced to about half, add the remaining sherry and soy sauce, the optional monosodium glutamate, and the cornstarch blended with 1 tablespoon of water. Stir gently for 30 to 40 seconds. Serve on a heated dish with plain boiled rice as an accompaniment.

❧

This dish is said to derive from a recipe over a thousand years old. It was recently discovered and has become a regular feature on the menu of the Hang Chow Restaurant in Hangchow, Chekiang.

Slice the pork into 20 thin slices, 2 inches by 1 inch. Cut the fatback into 20 pieces. Spread the slices of pork flat and let dry in a well ventilated place for 4 hours. Place a piece of fatback on top of each piece of pork. To make them stick together, hit them heavily with a mallet or the flat side of a Chinese cleaver. Place a shrimp on top of each one and gently hit again to flatten the shrimp against the fatback and the pork. Place each piece of garnished pork in a wire basket and deep-fry in hot oil for 45 seconds. Drain.

Heat the 3 tablespoons of sesame oil in a large skillet. Sauté the sweet pepper in it until it turns black. Remove the skillet from the heat and discard the pepper. Combine the sherry, soy sauce, wine-sediment paste, and optional monosodium glutamate. Arrange the pork in the skillet and sprinkle each piece with the sherry mixture. Place the skillet over high heat and fry the pork for 1 minute, basting with the juices in the skillet. Transfer the pork to a heated plate, arranging the pieces in a single layer, and serve.

Double-fried Eel

CH'AO PAO FANG

1 3–4 lb. skinned eel
3 tbs. sherry
vegetable oil for deep-frying
4 scallions
3 tbs. vegetable oil
1 tb. chopped fresh ginger root
3 tbs. soy sauce
1 tb. sugar
¼ tsp. five-spice powder

Riot of Spring

TUN T'SAI HO

3 medium heads of cabbage
  (about 5 lbs.)
1 chicken breast
1 thin slice cooked smoked ham
¼ cup bamboo shoots
8 dried Chinese mushrooms,
  soaked and drained
1 egg white
1 tsp. cornstarch
2 cups chicken bouillon
1 tsp. salt
1 tsp. monosodium glutamate
  (optional)
1 tb. chicken fat
vegetable oil for deep-frying
1 tb. dry sherry

When stewed, eel is ideal to eat with rice because of its richness. Eel is often quick-fried and treated as a light dish to accompany cocktails. In this recipe it is deep fried before it is quick-fried with other ingredients.

Blanch the eel in boiling water for 1 minute. Drain, dry, and rub with half the sherry. Place in a wire basket and deep-fry in the hot oil for 4 minutes. Drain, and cut the flesh of the eel neatly into 2-inch-by-1-inch strips, discarding the head and tail. Cut the scallions into 1-inch pieces.

Place the strips of eel in a wire basket and deep-fry again for 3 minutes, or until golden. (By this time there will probably be no more than 1 lb. of eel flesh left.) Drain. Heat the 3 tablespoons oil in a skillet. Add the remaining sherry, the scallions, ginger, soy sauce, sugar, and five-spice powder. Cook over high heat for 1 minute, stirring constantly. Add the eel strips. Baste and mix them with the sauce in the pan. Season with pepper to taste. Place on a heated dish and serve immediately.

❧

In this recipe a vegetable is presented as a separate dish, not merely as an accompaniment or garnish.

Cut off the stems of the cabbages. Remove and reserve the outer leaves until each heart stands out like an upstanding, firm green bud. Cut the chicken breast into thin slices, 1 inch by ½ inch. Slice the ham and bamboo shoots in the same manner. Cut the mushrooms into ¼-inch-wide strips. Mix the egg white and cornstarch in a bowl and dip the sliced chicken in it.

Bring the chicken bouillon to a boil in a large pan. Add half the salt, half the optional monosodium glutamate, and half the chicken fat. Place the cabbage hearts and leaves in this mixture and boil for 1 to 1½ minutes.

Remove the cabbage and arrange the leaves to line the sides of a deep ovenproof dish or casserole, reserving the hearts. Pack the middle of the casserole with 3 or 4 layers of tender leaves from the hearts. Deep-fry the chicken slices for 45 seconds. Arrange them, along with the ham, bamboo shoots, and mushrooms, in concentric rings on top of the layers of green leaves. Pour in the bouillon and dot with the remaining chicken fat. Sprinkle with the remaining salt, monosodium glutamate, and the sherry. Place in a steamer, cover, and steam for 25 minutes. Serve in the casserole.

Sea cucumber is a delicacy in China. It is eaten more for its texture than for its taste.

Scrub the sea cucumber gently with a hard brush to clean. Soak for 24 hours in warm water, changing the water several times. Clean carefully, remove the internal organs, and then rinse in fresh water. Blanch in boiling water for 3 minutes, drain, and set aside. Reserve the egg yolks for another dish and cut the whites into thin slices. Cut the ham and the cooked chicken breast into 1-inch-long, thin, flat slices. Blend the cornstarch and optional monosodium glutamate with the 3 tablespoons of water and mix with the bean sprouts.

Make several slashes on the meat of the pork hocks. Blanch the hocks and uncooked chicken in boiling water for 3 minutes. Drain, and place them in a saucepan. Add the 3¾ cups water, half the ginger, half the sherry, and half the scallions. Bring to a boil and simmer gently for 3 hours. Strain the broth and set aside.

Heat the lard in a skillet. Add the remaining ginger and scallions. Sauté these for 2 minutes and then discard. Lower the sea cucumber gently into the hot lard and sauté for 1 minute. Turn over once and add the egg whites, ham, cooked chicken breast, remaining sherry, reserved broth, and salt. Lower the heat and simmer for 15 minutes. Add the bean sprout mixture. Bring to a boil and after 1 minute of simmering, transfer to a large tureen and serve.

Chinese cuisine traditionally combines the fresh and young with the old and dried or salted. If the special Shao Hsing pickles, often eaten with this dish, are unavailable substitute chutney or pickles or even salted sauerkraut.

Cut the pork through the skin so that each piece will have skin attached into pieces, 1½ inches by 1 inch by 1 inch. Rinse the cabbage in water once and let drain and dry. Place the pork in a pan and add the water, soy sauce, sugar, and sherry. Bring to a boil and simmer for 30 minutes.

Add the salted cabbage. Continue to simmer for 5 minutes. Place half the salted cabbage at the bottom of a bowl with the pork on top, skinside down. Arrange the remaining cabbage on top of the pork and pour over the liquid from the pan. Cover and steam for 2½ hours. Transfer the contents of the bowl into a deep serving dish.

Butterfly Sea Cucumber

HU T'IEH HAI SHEN

1 lb. sea cucumber
2 hard-boiled eggs
1 slice cooked smoked ham
½ small cooked chicken breast
1 tsp. cornstarch
½ tsp. monosodium glutamate (optional)
3 tbs. water
1 tb. bean sprouts
½ lb. pork hocks
½ lb. raw chicken
3¾ cups water
4 slices fresh ginger root
3 tbs. dry sherry
6 scallions
2 tbs. lard
½ tsp. salt

Steamed Pork with Salted Cabbage

KAN T'SAI MEN JOU

1½ lbs. pork, fresh picnic shoulder or loin roast (with skin and at least three layers of fat and lean meat)
1 cup Chinese salted cabbage
1¾ cups water
2 tbs. soy sauce
1 tb. sugar
1 tb. dry sherry

Vegetable Rice

T'SAI FAN

3½ cups long-grain rice
1 medium cabbage (about 1½ lbs.)
2 tbs. lard
2 tsps. salt
2½ cups cold water
⅔ cup boiling water

This recipe, from the Mei Yee Chai Restaurant in Shanghai, is such a plain and simple dish that rich, spicy food is usually eaten with it.

Wash the rice and let it soak in cold water for 3 hours. Clean the cabbage thoroughly; remove and discard the coarse outer leaves and stems. Cut the cabbage leaves into 1-inch squares.

Heat the lard in a large heavy saucepan. When it is very hot, add the cabbage. Reduce the heat and stir-fry gently for 3 minutes; then add the salt and the cold water. Turn the heat to high. When the water starts to boil, add the rice. Continue to stir gently with a wooden spoon until the water reboils. Then lower the heat and cover tightly. When the water has nearly all been absorbed by the rice (after 10 to 12 minutes), pour in the boiling water. Poke 4 holes through the rice to the bottom of the pan to facilitate steaming. Cover firmly and place an asbestos mat underneath the pan. After 5 minutes, remove the pan from the heat. Allow the rice to steam in its own heat for 10 minutes.

Being highly spiced, this dish is excellent accompanied by vegetable rice.

Cut the meat into 6 pieces and boil in the water for 20 minutes. Remove the pork and cut the pieces into slices 2½ inches by 1 inch (each piece should have skin attached).

Skim the liquid and reserve half of it, discarding the remainder. Place the pork in a heavy pan or casserole and add the reserved liquid. Add the onion, ginger, tangerine peel, sugar, and soy sauce. Bring to a boil, cover, and simmer gently for 1½ hours. Alternatively, if you are using a casserole you might prefer to cook this dish in a preheated 350 oven for the same amount of time. The pork should be served in a heated bowl or tureen.

Pork of Four Happinesses

SSU HSI JOU

3 lbs. pork, fresh picnic shoulder
   or loin roast, with skin
6¼ cups water
3 tbs. chopped onion
3 slices fresh ginger root
1 tb. dried tangerine (or orange)
   peel
3 tbs. sugar
¼ cup soy sauce ·

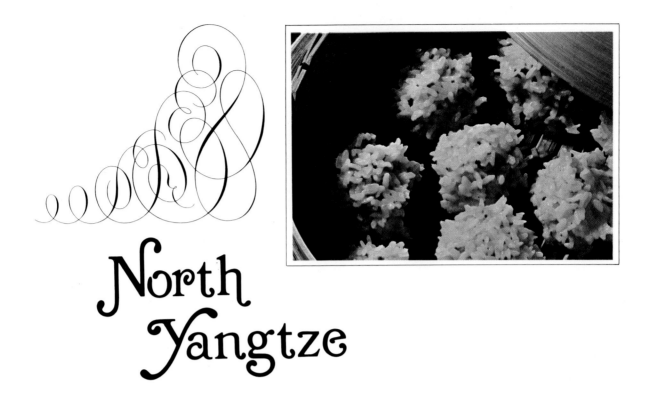

North Yangtze

The area north of the Yangtze is very much tougher than the areas south of the river. Most of the rougher manual work South-of-the-River seems to be performed by men who have migrated to find work in the larger towns and cities. Northern Kiangsu and the province of Anhwei (which covers approximately fifty four thousand square miles, with a population of over thirty three million) were important rice-producing regions, but because they were situated between the Yellow River and the Yangtze, they were greatly affected by drought and flood. The inhabitants of the area saw days of comparative affluence alternated with days of downright famine.

Kiangsu province is studded with lakes, rivers, and canals, all off-shoots of the Yangtze River. These waters yield a plentiful supply of shad, sole, mullet, crabs, and shrimp (which, incidentally, are eaten live). There is such an abundance of freshwater food that fish finds its way into many of the regional dishes, in combination with other foods. In Hofei, for instance—which is situated midway between the Yangtze and Yellow Rivers—there is an interesting lamb-fish dish called "Fish Eats Lamb." Fish and gravy over noodles is another provincial specialty.

Historically, the area has produced a good sprinkling of cultivated politicians and men of letters (as well as hordes of outlaws and refugees). These small groups of cultured and cultivated people were probably responsible for some of the surprisingly well-devised and delicate dishes that are produced and eaten in towns like Yangchow and Hofei. Especially tasty is the dainty meat-filled mushroom dish from Hofei that is usually served as an appetizer, before a multicourse dinner.

Yangchow is particularly famous for the delicacy of its noodles and the deliciousness of its hot pastries. Again, daintiness in size and shape is characteristic of the foods prepared by the people of this area, who seem to prefer everything bite-size. Even the spareribs are prepared as miniature chops.

A great deal of artistry is reflected in the way foods are arranged and served. Floral patterns prevail, giving even the simplest dish stature and grace. Feasts are always preceded by splendid assortments of hors d'oeuvres, so beautifully designed on the platters that several minutes must be devoted to admiring before eating them.

Small, one-bite-size juicy buns, filled with cabbage and pork, are a culinary favorite of the region. Kiangsu cuisine generally is inclined to be sweeter than that of other provinces. Even the salty dishes have a lot of sweetening in them.

Fried rice is, of course, a national specialty, and each region lends its own particular touch to the dish. The deluxe Yangchow version has achieved not only national, but international, fame. Because no soy sauce is used, it has a very delicate flavor—just right for topping off a banquet of rich food. The Chinese usually serve it as a last course at a formal meal.

Yangchow is well known, too, for sizzling fried-rice toast, a simple but surprisingly delectable dish. (Rice toast is the crunchy, almost burned bottom layer of rice, which, when good and dry, is deep-fried and dropped into soup, making a sizzling sound.) Another specialty of the city is its version of the dish known as Lion's Head—a large meatball, full of tasty ingredients, with a mantle of cooked cabbage leaves.

The southern reaches of the Central Plain of North China are marked by hundreds of miles of featureless plains, somewhat like America's Midwest. When the harvest is good, Wu-Hu, the port on the Yangtze, is one of the greatest rice-marketing centers of China.

The cooks of Wu-Hu, a center of gastronomy, specialize in fish dishes. Mullet, perch, and steamed shad are most popular here, and are eaten either plain or with soy sauce.

Plentiful grain cereals in good years must have accounted for the wide availability of swine and poultry, which are well represented in the diet of the region. One of the delicacies here is smoked duck's tongue. There is also a wide range of fresh vegetables.

The use of lamb and mutton is a practice that originated in the North. This is certainly an area that overlaps both the North and the South. Tripe, a popular food throughout China, is eaten extensively in this region, and tripe soup typifies the provincial cuisine.

The people of the North Yangtze area seem to drink more tea and wine than the Chinese of other regions. They like to nibble on tasty tidbits while sipping their drinks. A favorite combination is crabs and wine, and a helping of fine bean curd slivers makes an excellent companion for the beverages drunk here.

The dishes of this region clearly reflect the inevitable influence of geography on the food and culinary habits of the people.

Garnished Steamed Sole

CH'ING CHENG PIEN YÜ

2 soles, about 1 lb. each
2 tsps. salt
¼ cup dry sherry
3 tbs. chicken bouillon
1½ tsps. sugar
½ tsp. monosodium glutamate
    (optional)
1 tb. lard

FOR THE GARNISH:
1 tb. diced fatback
1½ tsps. sugar
2 slices smoked ham
¼ cup bamboo shoots
2 scallions
12 small dried Chinese
    mushrooms, soaked and
    drained
8 slices fresh ginger root

When cooking is done by plain steaming, the flavor depends—as it does in this dish—on marinating and garnishing. This recipe comes from the Ren Hua Lo Restaurant in Shanghai.

Clean the fish thoroughly and dry well. Rub both sides with the salt and half the sherry. Cut 3 slashes on each side of the soles, halfway through the flesh. Place them on an oval ovenproof dish. Heat the bouillon then add to it the remaining sherry, sugar, optional monosodium glutamate, and the lard; mix well. Sprinkle this mixture evenly over the fish. To make the garnish, pile half the diced fatback and sugar in the middle of each fish. Cut the ham and bamboo shoots into thin 2-inch strips and cut the scallions into 1-inch segments. Use the ham and bamboo shoots to form 2 lines at right angles to each other, meeting at the middle. Put the scallions, mushrooms, and ginger in the spaces. Cover and steam over high heat for 20 minutes. Wipe the edge of the dish with a cloth and bring directly to the table.

Tripe Soup

CH'ING TUN TU TZU T'ANG

¾ lb. precooked tripe
1 tb. salt
2 tbs. lard
3 slices fresh ginger root
1 tb. chopped onion
1 tb. chopped scallion
2 cups water
1 tsp. sesame oil
1 tsp. monosodium glutamate
    (optional)

Braised tripe and tripe soup are popular dishes in China. Here is a simple tripe soup as it is prepared by the Municipal Catering Company of Wu-han.

Wash the tripe 3 or 4 times in fresh water. Rub with 2 teaspoons of the salt and set aside for 10 minutes. Plunge the tripe in boiling water and simmer for 20 minutes. Rinse under running water and then slice into strips, 1½ inches by ½ inch.

Heat the lard in a skillet. Stir-fry the ginger, onion, and scallion in it for 1 minute. Add the tripe and continue to stir-fry gently for 5 to 6 minutes. Add the remaining salt and the water. Then transfer the contents to an ovenproof pot or casserole. Cover and simmer over very low heat or cook in a preheated 350 oven for 2 hours. Season with salt to taste and add the sesame oil and optional monosodium glutamate. Serve in the casserole.

Meat-filled Mushrooms

HSIANG KU HO

30 large Chinese dried
  mushrooms
¼ lb. lean pork
2 tbs. cooked smoked ham
1 egg
1 tb. chopped onion
1 tb. ground dried shrimp
1 tb. cornstarch
1½ tsps. soy sauce

FOR THE SAUCE:
1½ tsps. soy sauce
⅔ cup chicken bouillon
2 tsps. cornstarch
½ tsp. monosodium glutamate
  (optional)
1 tb. lard

This recipe comes from Chef Pei Hsiung Pan of Hofei, Anhwei. It is a dainty and savory introductory dish for a multicourse dinner.

Remove the stems from the mushrooms; soak the caps in warm water for 30 minutes. Grind the pork and ham and mix in a bowl with the egg, onion, shrimp, cornstarch, soy sauce, and a pinch of salt. Spread the mixture over the inside of 15 of the mushroom caps and cover each one with a second mushroom cap. Put a board over them and press gently to flatten, keeping the insides of the caps together sandwichlike. Arrange the mushrooms on a large plate. Place in a steamer, cover, and steam for 20 minutes. Meanwhile, prepare the sauce by mixing the soy sauce, and chicken bouillon with the cornstarch, optional monosodium glutamate, and a pinch of salt. Bring to a boil and add the lard, stirring a few times to blend. Pour the sauce over the mushrooms and serve immediately.

Frosted Spareribs

KUA SHUANG P'AI KU

1 lb. lean spareribs
3 egg whites
⅔ cup cornstarch
vegetable oil for deep-frying
6 tbs. water
½ preserved kumquat
½ cup sugar

These miniature chops are obtained by chopping lean spareribs across the bone, to about an inch or less in length. This dish is served cold.

Separate the spareribs. Then chop them into pieces of about ½- to 1-inch long. Mix the egg whites in a bowl with the cornstarch. Add the chops and mix well. Then place them in batches in a finemeshed wire basket and deep-fry in hot oil for 3 to 4 minutes. Remove from the oil and drain.

Heat the water in a pan. Cut the kumquat into 4 pieces and add, along with the sugar. Boil for 30 seconds. Add the fried chops, turning them in the pan until they are thoroughly coated with syrup. Pour the contents of the pan into a large bowl to cool. When cool, place in the refrigerator. When the chops are quite cold, they become encrusted with white sugar; hence they are "frosted."

A good introductory dish for a multicourse Chinese dinner, these scallops are deep fried and crispy. Plum sauce and Haisein sauce are often served with this lamb.

Boil the lamb for 1 minute in water to cover; then simmer gently for 12 minutes. Drain the lamb and slice into thin pieces, 2 inches by 1 inch. Cut the scallions into 1-inch pieces. Place the lamb in a bowl with the scallions, ginger, chili pepper, optional monosodium glutamate, and sesame oil. Marinate for 20 minutes. Beat the eggs in another bowl and blend with the cornstarch.

Remove the lamb from the marinade and, using your fingers, coat thoroughly with the cornstarch and egg mixture. Place the pieces of lamb in a wire basket and deep-fry in hot oil for 3 minutes, or until golden. Cut each piece into 3 strips and serve on a heated place.

> This dish makes an excellent and unusual hot hors d'oeuvre to be served with cocktails. The meat can be prepared and coated in advance, then kept refrigerated. For best results, allow meat to remain at room temperature for one half hour before deep-frying.

🍃

In Hofei, Anhwei, which is about midway between the Yangtze and the Yellow rivers, one finds this dish which combines lamb with fish. It is, in fact, a casserole of fish with lamb as stuffing.

Clean the fish thoroughly. Chop the lamb into pieces, about 1 inch by ½ inch. Boil in water to cover for 1 minute. Then drain and rub with the salt. Stuff the fish with the lamb and 2 slices of the ginger. Rub the suet on both sides with cornstarch and wrap the fish in it—if necessary secure with wooden toothpicks.

Place the suet-wrapped fish in a wire basket and deep-fry in hot oil for 7 to 8 minutes, turning it over once or twice. Drain the fish; remove and discard the suet. Then place the fish in an oval ovenproof casserole. Pour in the chicken bouillon. Add the remaining ginger, sugar, scallions, aniseed, soy sauce, and wine. Cover and simmer for 1 hour.

Serve the fish, garnished with the parsley, in the casserole in which it was cooked.

Deep-fried Lamb

CHIAO CHA YANG JOU

¾ lb. lean lamb, cut from the leg
6 scallions
1 tsp. chopped fresh ginger root
1 tsp. dried chili pepper
½ tsp. monosodium glutamate (optional)
1 tb. sesame oil
3 eggs
½ cup cornstarch
vegetable oil for deep-frying
plum sauce
Haisein sauce

Fish "Eats" Lamb

YÜ YAO YANG

1 2–3 lb. carp or bass
½ lb. lamb
1 tsp. salt
4 slices fresh ginger root
1 strip of beef suet
¼ cup cornstarch
vegetable oil for deep-frying
3¾ cups chicken bouillon
1 tb. sugar
2 scallions
1 tsp. aniseed
3 tbs. soy sauce
⅔ cup red wine
2 tbs. minced parsley

85

Steamed Beef in Rice Flour

FENG CHENG NIU JOU

1¾ lbs. beef tenderloin
⅓ cup ginger water
2 tbs. vegetable oil
1 tb. dry sherry
2 tb. soy sauce
1 tb. fermented black beans,
   soaked for 1 hour
1½ tsps. sugar
1 tsp. chili sauce
½ cup rice flour
crushed coriander seeds
bay leaves
chopped chives
fresh thyme

In all other parts of China, pork is usually served with rice flour. In the North Yangtze region, beef is used.

Cut the meat into pieces, 1½ inches by ¾ inch by ½ inch. Place the meat in a bowl and add the ginger water, oil, sherry, soy sauce, black beans, sugar, and chili sauce. Work the mixture into the meat with your fingers. Finally, dry-fry the rice flour until it begins to turn brown. Coat the pieces of meat with the rice flour.

Divide the meat among 4 ovenproof bowls. To the first bowl, add a few coriander seeds, to the second, add a few bay leaves, to the third, a few chives, to the fourth, a little thyme. Place the four bowls in a steamer, cover, and steam for 30 minutes. Serve with rice.

The areas around the Tunting Lake produce a breed of pig, the flesh of which is noted for its tenderness. The best glutinous rice comes from the Liu Yang county of Hunan. It is from these two basic materials that this recipe is created.

Wash the rice 3 times and soak in cold water for 1 hour. Drain well and spread on a baking sheet or sheet of wax paper. Grind the lean pork. Blanch the fatback in water for 5 minutes, drain, and cut into pea-sized pieces. Cut the water chestnuts into pieces of the same size.

Place the pork in a bowl and add the salt, pepper, optional monosodium glutamate, eggs, sherry, and cornstarch blended with the water. Mix well. Then add the fatback, scallions, water chestnuts, and ginger. Form the mixture into meatballs, ½ inch in diameter. Roll them in the rice; when covered, press the rice firmly into the meatballs.

Arrange the rice-covered meatballs in not more than 2 layers in a large ovenproof dish. Cover with foil and steam vigorously for 20 minutes. These rice-pork "pearls," should be brought steaming to the table. They are best eaten dipped in soy sauce.

Steamed Rice-Pork Pearls

CHENG MI FEN YUAN TZU

1 cup short-grain rice
1¼ lbs. lean pork, arm steak or
   fresh ham center slice
¾ lb. fatback
8 water chestnuts
2 tsps. salt
¼ tsp. pepper
1 tsp. monosodium glutamate
   (optional)
3 eggs
1 tb. dry sherry
2 tbs. cornstarch
6 tbs. water
4 scallions, chopped
2 tsps. chopped fresh ginger root

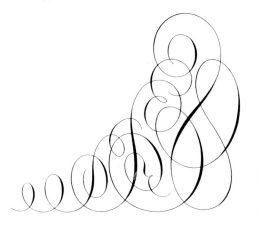

Mid-Yangtze

The mid-Yangtze region has sometimes been called the Rice Bowl of China, since the three provinces included here—Hupeh, Hunan, and Kiangsi—are rice-producing areas. It is also known as the Great Lake region of China. These large pools of water are practically continuous with the Yangtze, and act as natural reservoirs for the great river. The Tunting Lake in Hunan reaches seventy-five miles in length and fifty-five miles in width during the summer rains, and Kiangsi's Poyang Lake grows to eighty-five miles long and twenty miles wide. The combined population of the three provinces exceeds seventy-two million.

The province of Kiangsi (meaning "West of the River") is very hilly, with valleys that support an extensive population. Apart from developing rice, tea, coal, and tungsten, Kiangsi is the most famous source of porcelain, producing some of the most exquisite ware in all of China.

The bulk of the world's finest china comes from the small town of Ching Têh Chêng in Kiangsi. The products of this small, remote town are those which, for centuries, have stocked the great stately homes of Britain, France, and other countries. Today this china fetches fabulous prices in the famous auction rooms of the world.

The country's everyday spoon is made of porcelain, for very practical reasons: The material is a poor conductor of heat—a comfortable consideration for soup-loving Chinese lips. Also, because it is nonmetallic, there is no danger that the character of delicate foods will be changed in any way.

On the peaks of Kiangsi's highest mountains is grown a delicious green tea called (poetically and appropriately) "Cloud Mist Tea." Because the mountaintops are too high for even experienced climbers, monkeys are recruited and trained to be tea-leaf pickers. According to provincial legend, the agile little animals carry baskets which they fill with the plucked leaves and bring down to the waiting workers.

Nanchang was dubbed Kiangsi's "swinging capital" in A.D. 600 by a sixteen-year-old poet. His descriptive essay, "Ode to the Teng Huang Pavilion," staggered the literary world of the day and has since been accepted as one of the best writings of its type in Chinese literature. A chicken dish flavored with ginger and tangerines has since become known as "Swinging Chicken."

The people from the province of Hunan (which means "South of the Lake") are tough and renowned as fighters. During the Taiping Rebellion of the mid-nineteenth century, the Manchu Dynasty, with the help of General Gordon, recruited the bulk of the mercenaries from this region to suppress the Rebellion. One of the more famous "products" of Hunan province is Mao Tse-tung, born to a peasant family there in 1893.

The natives of Hunan enjoy rich-tasting dishes, and like their food hot and spicy. Hot pepper is an important seasoning in the dishes of these provinces, as it is in Szechwan; chili is used in almost every other dish. Food is characteristically served in huge vessels and eaten with extra-long chopsticks—so long, in fact, that the Hunanese allegedly feed each other across the table, it supposedly being too difficult to bring the ends of their chopsticks to their own mouths!

Although it is predominantly mountainous and wooded, Hunan is generously marked with streams, so that its valleys are extremely fertile and vegetables grow in abundance. In the Tunting Lake region, a special kind of pig is bred, prized throughout the province for its tenderness.

Wu-Han (or the twin cities of Wuchan and Hankow) is the capital of Hupeh, the third province of this region. It is the largest metropolis of the region, and is situated at the crossroads between the east-west communication along the Yangtze and the north-south communication along the Peking-Canton railway. It is gradually developing into one of the most important industrial complexes in the country.

It was at Wu-Han that the only bridge that spanned the Yangtze—a double-decker—was opened with great pride a few years ago. The size of the area and its population would lead one to expect a great culinary output. But the whole area, being the geographical center of China, appears to have been so heavily awash in political turmoil and warfare during the past half-century or more that there have been few establishments of permanence where culinary art could develop and prosper.

The industrial tempo of Wu-Han is probably responsible for the efficiency of its cuisine. In more typical Chinese towns, with their unhurried approach to cooking (and living in general), it would take at least three times longer to cook some of these dishes.

The dishes of character and individuality that are produced in this area are definitely more limited than those of any of the other areas of corresponding size and population.

Quick-fried Chicken

WEN SHAN CHI T'ING

2 large chicken breasts
½ cup bamboo shoots
1 small red sweet pepper,
    trimmed and seeded
1 scallion
1½ tsps. dried chili peppers
1 tsp. salt
1 egg
1 tb. cornstarch
¼ cup vegetable oil
2 tbs. lard
⅓ cup chicken bouillon
1 tb. dry sherry
½ tsp. monosodium glutamate
    (optional)
1 tb. light colored soy sauce
1 tsp. sesame oil

The sweet pepper and chili peppers give this chicken a delicious piquant flavor.

Cut the chicken breasts into ¼-inch cubes. Cut the bamboo shoots and the sweet pepper into similar-sized pieces. Slice the scallion into ¼-inch pieces. Chop the chili peppers and discard the seeds.

Place the diced chicken in a bowl. Add the salt and rub it into the chicken. Break the egg into the bowl and mix well. Then blend in the cornstarch. Heat the vegetable oil in a large skillet. When quite hot, pour in the chicken and stir-fry for 1½ minutes. Remove the chicken and discard any remaining oil. Add the lard to the skillet. Stir-fry the bamboo shoots, sweet pepper, and the chili peppers over high heat for 2 minutes. Mix the chicken bouillon with the sherry and add along with the optional monosodium glutamate, soy sauce, and sesame oil. Stir-fry gently for 30 seconds. Add the pieces of chicken and continue to stir-fry for another 30 seconds. Transfer to a heated dish and serve.

Soy-braised Fish

HUANG MEN YÜ

1½ lb. fish fillets (bass, carp,
    halibut, or cod)
1 tsp. salt
4 scallions
vegetable oil for deep-frying
2 tbs. lard
4 slices fresh ginger root
1 tsp. dried chili pepper
1 tb. soy sauce
3 tbs. dry sherry
½ tsp. monosodium glutamate
    (optional)
1 tsp. sesame oil

The farther one travels up the Yantze, the less sugar is found in this traditional recipe, until it disappears entirely from the ingredients.

Chop the fish into 1-inch cubes. Rub evenly with the salt, using your fingers. Cut the scallions into pieces 1 inch long. Heat the vegetable oil and deep-fry the fish for 2 minutes. Drain thoroughly.

Heat the lard in a skillet, and sauté the ginger and chili pepper for 30 seconds. Add the fish and turn it over in the lard a couple of times. Pour in the soy sauce and sherry. Turn the fish over several times and cover the skillet. Simmer the contents over low heat for 3 minutes. Remove the lid and sprinkle the fish with the optional monosodium glutamate and sesame oil. Add the scallions. Bring to the table on a heated serving dish.

Toss-fried Rice Noodles

CH'AO MI FEN

1½ lbs. rice stick noodles
½ lb. lean pork
1 cup dried Chinese mushrooms,
  soaked and drained
½ cup bamboo shoots
½ celery stalk
1 small leek
¼ cup lard
2 cloves garlic, crushed
3 tbs. soy sauce
⅔ cup chicken bouillon or
  superior broth
1 tsp. monosodium glutamate
  (optional)

The frying of noodles in lard and meat juice makes them savory and appealing to lovers of pasta. The use of crunchy textures such as bamboo shoots and celery, soft materials like mushrooms and noodles, and aromatic ingredients such as leeks and garlic creates an interesting contrast in texture, aroma, and taste.

Place the noodles in a pan of boiling water and boil gently until soft and cooked, 5 to 10 minutes. Drain and cool under cold running water; then set aside.

Slice the pork, mushrooms, bamboo shoots, celery, and leek into matchstick-thin strips.

Heat three-quarters of the lard in a skillet over high heat. Add the pork and bamboo shoots; stir-fry for 30 seconds and then add the mushrooms, leek, and garlic. Fry for 1 minute. Add the celery, soy sauce, bouillon, and optional monosodium glutamate. Simmer for 2 minutes. Remove from the heat and place the contents of the pan in a bowl.

Add the remaining lard to the skillet. Place over medium heat for 30 seconds. Then add the cooked noodles. Stir-fry gently for 3 minutes. Add half the pork mixture and all its liquid. Continue to stir-fry for 2 minutes. By this time, the noodles should have absorbed all the liquid. Turn the contents onto a large, flat, heated serving dish. Heat the remaining pork mixture in the skillet over high heat for 1 minute and use it as a garnish or topping for the noodles.

❧

Peppered Chicken

HUA CHIAO CHI

1 2–2½ lb. chicken or chicken
  pieces
6 scallions
2 slices fresh ginger root
1 tb. soy sauce
1 tb. vinegar
1 tsp. salt
2 tbs. sesame oil
2 tsps. dried red chili peppers

The combination of sesame oil and chili peppers in this dish gives the chicken an individual and interesting taste.

Plunge the chicken into boiling water to cover and simmer for 10 minutes. Chop into pieces, about 1 inch by ½ inch, including the bones. Arrange the pieces in a large ovenproof dish, skinside down. Cut the scallions into ½-inch pieces. Add the scallions and ginger to the chicken. Mix the soy sauce, vinegar, and salt in a bowl.

Heat the sesame oil in a small skillet, and sauté the chili peppers in it for 2 to 3 minutes. Discard the peppers and pour the oil evenly over the chicken in the ovenproof dish. Then pour the soy sauce mixture over the chicken. Place in a steamer, cover, and steam for 30 to 35 minutes. Serve the chicken on a large heated serving dish.

Wu-Han is an industrial center and the dishes produced here are more efficient than elaborate. If this dish had been prepared in a town of greater leisureliness, it would probably take three times as long to cook!

Chop the pork into pieces 1½ inches long by 1 inch wide by ¼ inch thick, discarding any skin. Cut the carrots into wedge-shaped pieces as shown below.

Heat the lard in a skillet and sauté the pork for 4 minutes over high heat. Add the carrots and broth. Bring to a boil and simmer for 5 minutes. Add the garlic with the sherry, soy sauce, onion, leek, salt, and ginger. Reboil and simmer for 10 minutes. Add the optional monosodium glutamate, cornstarch blended with a little water, and pepper to taste. Bring to a boil and cook for 1 minute. Transfer to a heated dish and serve.

Red-cooked Pork with Carrots

LO PO SHAO JOU

1½ lbs. pork, fresh shoulder or
   loin
4 medium carrots
1½ tbs. lard
2½ cups secondary broth
2 cloves garlic, crushed
3 tbs. dry sherry
3 tbs. soy sauce
1 tb. chopped onion
1 tb. chopped leek
½ tsp. salt
3 slices fresh ginger root
1 tsp. monosodium glutamate
   (optional)
1 tb. cornstarch

Hold the knife blade straight up and down and at a 45 degree angle to the carrot. Roll the carrot one-quarter turn after each slice.

93

Snails in Wine-Sediment Paste

TSAO YU LUO

6-12 fresh snails per person
5 tsps. wine-sediment paste
½ cup water
¼ lb. bacon rind in one piece
6 scallions
¼ cup lard
6 slices fresh ginger root
⅓ cup dry sherry
⅓ cup soy sauce
2½ cups water
½ tsp. monosodium glutamate
   (optional)
¼ tsp. pepper
few sprigs parsley

As in France, snails are a delicacy in China. Cooked in wine-sediment paste, they are superb.

To wash and clean the snails, cut off the pointed end of the shell. Scrub them and then soak in fresh water for 24 hours. Rinse under cold water in a colander.

Mix the wine-sediment paste with the ½ cup water and beat it with a pair of chopsticks for 30 seconds. Strain into a bowl. Cut the bacon rind into 1-inch squares. Cut the scallions into 2-inch pieces. Heat half the lard in a heavy pan and sauté the scallions and ginger for 1 minute. Add the snails and stir-fry for 2 minutes. Add half the sherry, the soy sauce, and the 2½ cups of water. Bring to a boil and simmer for 4 minutes.

Remove the snails from the pan and skim the surface of the liquid. Return the snails to the liquid. Add the wine-sediment paste, bacon rind, remaining lard, remaining sherry, the optional monosodium glutamate, and the pepper. Simmer for 4 minutes. Strain the sauce. Because there is ample sauce, the snails should be served in a deep plate. Garnish with a few sprigs of parsley and serve steaming hot.

Vegetables grow in abundance in this part of China. For the sake of tenderness, often only the heart of cabbage is used. The outer leaves are fed to the pigs so that nothing is wasted. Salt beef could be substituted for pork in this dish.

Cut the meat into paper-thin slices, 1½ inches long and ½-inch wide. Remove and discard the outer leaves and bottom of the cabbage, leaving only the tender inside leaves. Cut these crisscross into 2-inch pieces.

Heat the oil in a skillet over high heat. When very hot, add the cabbage and scramble-fry for 1½ minutes. Add the pork and bouillon. Sprinkle with the salt and optional monosodium glutamate. Stir-fry gently for 3 minutes. Add the lard and after a couple of stirs and tosses, transfer to a heated dish and serve.

Salt Pork with Cabbage Heart

YEN JOU T'SAI HSIN

¼ lb. salt pork or salt beef
1 cabbage (about 1½ lbs.)
3 tbs. vegetable oil
⅓ cup chicken bouillon
1 tsp. salt
½ tsp. monosodium glutamate (optional)
1 tb. lard

Swinging Chicken

HUNG TU CHI

1 2–2½ lb. chicken, or chicken pieces
3 tbs. dark soy sauce
1 small leek
3 tbs. dried tangerine (or orange) peel, soaked and drained
¾ cup lard
4 tsps. chopped fresh ginger root
2 tsps. dried red chili peppers, seeded and chopped
1 tsp. sugar
1 tb. vinegar
1 tb. Haisein sauce
1 tb. dry sherry
1 tsp. monosodium glutamate (optional)
3 tbs. superior broth
½ tsp. pepper
1 tb. sesame oil

Hung Tu is the Chinese literary expression for the "Swinging Capital," and Nanchang, capital city of the Kiangsi Province, was first called this by a 16-year-old poet of the Sui dynasty (A.D. 600). The Hung Tu chicken is, therefore, the "Swinging Chicken" of Nanchang.

Clean the chicken and chop into 1-inch cubes, including the bones. Add the soy sauce and marinate for 5 minutes. Cut the leek into ½-inch segments. Slice the tangerine peel into matchstick-thin strips. Drain the chicken, reserving the soy sauce.

Heat the lard in a large skillet. Add the chicken and stir-fry in the hot lard over high heat for 3 to 4 minutes. Drain the chicken and discard all but 1 tablespoon of the lard. Add the ginger, chili peppers, leek, and tangerine peel. Stir-fry for 50 seconds. Return the chicken to the skillet. Add the reserved soy sauce, sugar, vinegar, Haisein sauce, sherry, optional monosodium glutamate, and broth. Continue to stir-fry for 3 to 4 minutes over high heat, or until the liquid in the skillet has been reduced to a thick sauce. Sprinkle with the pepper and sesame oil and serve in a heated dish.

This dish is in the Chinese tradition of the cooked salad, in which the crispy fish strips are mixed with crunchy celery and garnished with ham.

Cut the fish first into thin slices, then cut again into matchstick-thin strips about 2 inches long. Add the salt to the egg and beat well. Coat the fish with this mixture and dredge with the cornstarch. Wash the celery and cut into matchstick-thin strips. Plunge them into boiling water for 30 seconds; then drain. Add the soy sauce, sesame oil, and optional monosodium glutamate to the celery. Toss and mix well. Cut the ham into matchstick-thin strips.

Heat the oil in a deep-fryer. Using a frying basket add the fish and spread the pieces out evenly with a pair of bamboo chopsticks. Deep-fry for 3 to 4 minutes, after which time the strips of fish will float to the surface. Remove and drain them. Place the celery mixture in a large heated serving dish. Arrange the fried fish on top. Mix gently. Use the ham to garnish the fish and celery.

Fried Fish Strips

PAN YÜ KUA

1 lb. fish fillets (bass, haddock, pike, or cod)
1 tsp. salt
1 egg
2 tbs. cornstarch
1 small bunch celery
1 tb. light soy sauce
1 tsp. sesame oil
½ tsp. monosodium glutamate (optional)
1 small slice cooked, smoked ham
vegetable oil for deep-frying

Steamed Pork in Rice Flour

FEN CHENG JOU

½ lb. pork, fresh shoulder or loin
½ lb. fresh ham, center slice
1 tsp. salt
1 tb. soy sauce
1 tb. dry sherry
1 tb. red bean-curd cheese
4 slices fresh ginger root
1 tb. dried tangerine (or orange) peel, soaked and drained
½ tsp. monosodium glutamate (optional)
1½ tsps. sugar
⅓ cup rice flour
1½ cups dried sliced lotus roots, soaked and drained

The Chinese use rice flour in much the same way that Westerners use bread crumbs. To make the rice aromatic, it is browned for a short time over direct heat, until it turns golden yellow.

Cut the pork and ham into pieces, 1½ inches by ½ inch. Place in a bowl and mix well with the salt, soy sauce, sherry, red bean-curd cheese, ginger, tangerine peel, optional monosodium glutamate, sugar, and pepper to taste. Marinate for 2 hours or longer. Then roll the pork in the rice flour until completely coated.

Line an ovenproof casserole with the sliced lotus roots. Arrange the pork on top, place in a steamer, cover, and steam for 2 hours. Serve the pork in the casserole.

Sole in Cabbage Hearts

SHA YU T'SAI T'AI

1½ lbs. fillet of sole
1 tsp. salt
2 tsps. cornstarch
1 egg white
2 medium heads of young cabbage (about 2½ lbs.)
6 tbs. bamboo shoots
3 tbs. lard
⅔ cup chicken bouillon
¾ tsp. monosodium glutamate (optional)

In this recipe, the white of the fish and the green of the vegetable make for an attractive color combination, and the natural softness of both provides an interesting contrast in texture to accompanying dishes.

Cut the fish fillets into pieces, 2 inches by 1 inch. Mix half the salt with the cornstarch and egg white to form a batter. Coat the fish with this batter. Remove and discard all the outer leaves of the cabbages, leaving only the hearts. Cut each heart into quarters and again into 2-inch lengths. Thinly slice the bamboo shoots.

Heat the lard in a skillet. Add the pieces of fish and sauté for 1 minute on each side. Remove and drain. Add the cabbage to the skillet and sauté for 2 minutes. Then add the remaining salt, the bamboo shoots, and chicken bouillon. Simmer for 5 minutes. Return the fish to the skillet. Cover and simmer for 2 minutes. Sprinkle with the optional monosodium glutamate and pepper to taste.

Arrange the pieces of fish as neatly as possible on the cabbage on a heated plate and serve immediately.

Fukien

The province of Fukien covers an area of 47,500 square miles and has a population of nearly 15 million. Situated about halfway along the coast between Shanghai and Canton, it has a mountainous, jagged coastline with many bays, gulfs, inlets, and islands.

The climate here is semitropical, and fruits of all kinds abound. There are many tangerine orchards and a delicious variety of plum. Fruit is integral to this region's cuisine, appearing in many interesting combinations with meat and fish.

Fishing is an important industry here, and Fukien is famous for its excellent seafood dishes: oysters, clams, and varieties of fish. At the height of the season, the fishing junks sailing down the river to the open sea in fleets of several hundreds is a memorable sight. Because the Fukienese are partial to fish-flavored dishes, they make extensive use of a sauce made from shrimp. This sauce has a distinctive and pungent flavor, and it takes some time to develop a taste for it. It can be made from commercially sold shrimp paste, a heavy concentrate that must be used sparingly.

The province is famous for its soy sauce, reputedly the best in all of China. Its high quality is predominantly reflected in the cuisine in the "red cooking" of the region. (The phrase is derived from the fact that food cooked in soy sauce turns a rich red-brown color.) This method of cooking is a slower process than frying, and the people here prefer it in the preparation of large cuts of meat or whole chickens and duck, or certain kinds of fish (coarse-fleshed, usually).

Traditionally, the clever Chinese cook saves the leftover gravy from a red-cooked dish and uses it again to stew other foods. In time, the gravy takes on the personalities of the various foods cooked in it and grows richer-bodied with each use. Water is added as it is needed. Such a cooking sauce has a long, ever-enriched lifespan, and its age is something to brag about in the typical Chinese household.

Soups are another great specialty of the province, and the fish broth in particular is renowned. The varieties of soup are endless, but the common criterion is that they be clear and very tasty. (At dinner with a Fukienese friend in Malaya, there were seven dishes on the table—four of which were soups!)

Cooks of the region use a sweet-tasting red wine sediment paste as a cooking ingredient, a culinary touch for which Fukien is famous. The fermented rice paste enhances pork and chicken dishes especially.

Another provincial specialty is swallow-skin dough, made largely from meat that has been finely ground and mixed with cornstarch, then rolled on a board to form a dough. The swallow-skins are filled and folded, boiled, and served in soup. The Fukienese are fond of "wrapped" food generally. Soft spring rolls are a big favorite; the dough wrappers, very thin, are stuffed with many different kinds of vegetables and meats.

A traditional home-style dish of the region is *Popia*—an event in itself—which takes the family several days to prepare and several hours to sit around and enjoy. Again, it's basically a food-filled crêpe. The diner helps himself to one of the delicately thin crêpes (from a huge stack on the table), and daubs it with one or more of an assortment of sauces; he then spoons onto the center of the crêpe several globs of hot filling (consisting of pork, shrimp, vegetables, bean curd, and seasonings); then adds a sampling of various side dishes (dried seaweed, peanuts, parsley, bean sprouts, chives, and different relishes)—and the whole thing is rolled into a cylinder and eaten.

The people of this province have a penchant for shredding food—pork, fish, and the like. It requires endless patience; but the Chinese, who are steeped in the art of food appreciation, actually seem to enjoy all the painstaking preparation.

"Small eats" on the street is a popular provincial pastime. Food vendors are everywhere, servicing the insatiable on-the-spot eaters. The Chinese like a "little bowl of something" between meals. A typical street snack would be a bowl of thin vermicelli with a few slices of pork liver, done quickly to order in the vendor's hot stock-pot. This Chinese "barrow-boy" food can be quite distinctive and delicious, and is enjoyed by all classes of people.

Many of the province's mountainsides and hilltops are covered with tea plantations, which produce some of the best-known types of tea; the red ones especially are great. Indeed, before the 1870s, Foochow, the provincial capital, was one of the greatest tea ports in the world. It was from the Ming River that the famous China clippers used to set sail for London or Liverpool. Incidentally, Fukien is one of the few places where tea is served at dinner.

Green and White Soup

FEI CH'UI KENG

1½ lbs. fresh spinach
1 large chicken breast
2 tbs. cooked smoked ham
1 tsp. salt
1 tb. dry sherry
2 tsps. sugar
1 tsp. monosodium glutamate
  (optional)
2 tsps. cornstarch
6 egg whites
1 cup chicken bouillon
6 tbs. lard
½ tsp. chopped fresh ginger root
1 tsp. water

Swallow-Skin Soup

JOU YEN T'ANG

FOR THE SWALLOW-SKIN:
1½ lbs. lean pork
1 cup cornstarch

FOR THE FILLING:
1½ lbs. lean and fatty pork
1 cup cooked shelled shrimp
½ lb. water chestnuts
½ lb. bean curd (optional)
4-6 scallions
¼ cup soy sauce

FOR THE SOUP:
9 cups superior broth
4-6 scallions
1 tb. soy sauce
1 tsp. sesame oil
1 tsp. monosodium glutamate
  (optional)

Although called a soup, this is really more of a mousse, excellent ladled over rice.

Wash the spinach thoroughly and remove the stems; finely chop the leaves. Finely grind the chicken flesh and ham and place in a bowl. Add half the salt, half the sherry, half the sugar, half the optional monosodium glutamate, half the cornstarch, and the egg whites. Beat together for 1 minute. Add half the chicken bouillon and beat for an additional minute. Heat half the lard in a skillet. Add the spinach and the remaining salt, sherry, sugar, and optional monosodium glutamate, along with the ginger. Stir-fry for 3 minutes. Then add the remaining chicken bouillon. Stir-fry quickly and add the remaining cornstarch blended with the water. Pour into one half of a deep, flat-bottomed, oval serving dish.

Heat the remaining lard in another skillet and pour in the chicken and ham mixture. Stir-fry quickly for 2 minutes. Then pour it into the other half of the serving dish.

❧

Swallow-skin is a meat-based dough, unique to Fukien. It is formed into ravioli-like turnovers that are cooked in water and served in soup.

Make the swallow-skin dough by finely grinding the lean pork twice. Place it in a mortar, add the cornstarch, and pound them together. Mix thoroughly. Place the mixture on a board and roll it out to a thin sheet. Cut into 2-inch squares. To make the filling, finely grind the pork, shrimp, water chestnuts, optional bean curd, and the 4-6 scallions. Blend with the ¼ cup of soy sauce.

To wrap the filling in the dough, place a teaspoon of filling in the middle of each 2-inch square, held in the left palm. Fold the dough over with the thumb and fingers and press together to seal.

Place the swallow-skins in a large pan of water. Bring to a boil and simmer for 5 minutes. Drain and discard the water. Place swallow-skins in a large tureen. Heat the superior broth and pour into the tureen. Chop the remaining 4-6 scallions. Add the scallions, the 1 tb. soy sauce, sesame oil, optional monosodium glutamate, and pepper to taste. To serve, ladle the swallow-skins and soup into each individual bowl.

Clams in Chicken Broth

CHI T'ANG HAI PANG

4 lbs. clams in shells
1 1–1½ lb. chicken or chicken
    pieces
¼ lb. lean pork
1 slice fresh ginger root
3¾ cups water
3 tbs. dry sherry
1 tb. light soy sauce
¾ tsp. monosodium glutamate
    (optional)

> You can lightly bruise the slice
> of ginger root by hitting it with
> the back edge of a carving knife
> or cleaver. This will break the
> tough fibers and release the full
> flavor of the ginger.

Clams are considered a delicacy in Fukien. They have white flesh and are generally served very lightly cooked. This soup is usually served between quick-fried dishes to provide a break in variety and texture.

Cut away the body of the clam from its shell and clean the flesh thoroughly. Remove and discard the intestines. Halve the white flesh and soak in fresh water.

Chop the chicken through the bone into 4 pieces and slice the pork into 6 pieces. Place the chicken and pork in boiling water to cover and boil for 1½ minutes. Drain and discard the water. Pack the chicken and pork, with the ginger, in a deep ovenproof casserole or pot and pour in the 3¾ cups water. Cover and simmer, or steam in a steamer, for 2 hours. When the chicken-pork broth is ready, place the clams in a bowl. Cover with boiling water and soak for 45 seconds. Drain and discard the water. Add the sherry to the clams and marinate for 1 minute. Discard the marinade and place the clams in the bottom of a deep serving dish.

Remove the chicken and pork from the broth. The chicken and pork may be used in another recipe, if desired. Strain the broth and bring to a boil. Add the light soy sauce and optional monosodium glutamate. Pour the broth over the clams and serve immediately.

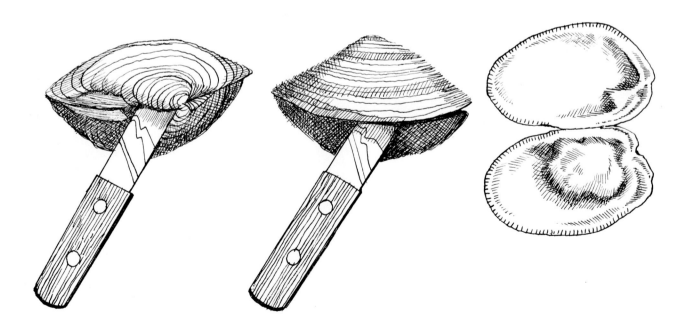

This dish is really a "small-eat" dish suitable to accompany cocktails or as a preliminary to a multicourse dinner.

Remove the chicken flesh from the bone and discard the skin. Finely chop the chicken flesh, fatback, shrimp, celery, and water chestnuts and then mix together in a bowl. Add the egg, half the salt, and half the optional monosodium glutamate. Spread out the chopped mixture to ½-inch thickness on a flat greased ovenproof plate. Place in a steamer, cover, and steam for 15 minutes. Remove from the steamer and slice into 1-inch by ½-inch by ⅛-inch thick slices. Arrange these on a plate, each leaning on the other in flower petal fashion.

Heat the broth in a small saucepan. Stir in the remaining salt and optional monosodium glutamate, the sesame oil, and the cornstarch blended with the water. Bring to a boil. Then pour it over the slices of chicken-shrimp mixture. Trim the red pepper, remove the seeds, and shred the flesh. Trim and shred the scallions, using the green part only. Trim the leeks and shred the white part finely, discarding the green tops. Garnish the plate with the shredded vegetables just before serving.

Red wine-sediment paste, produced in Fukien, is the principal flavoring of this chicken. The aromatic qualities of this dish and the rich red color make it especially appealing.

Chop the chicken into pieces, 1 inch by 1½ inches. Cut the bamboo shoots into similar-sized pieces and the white parts of the scallions into 1-inch segments. Heat the lard in a large skillet over high heat. Add the scallions, ginger, and wine-sediment paste. Then stir-fry for 1 minute. Add the chicken pieces and bamboo shoots and continue to stir-fry for 1 minute. Add the sugar, soy sauce, and sherry and continue stir-frying for 1 additional minute. Finally, pour in the bouillon. Bring to a boil and reduce the heat to low. Simmer for 35 minutes.

Lift the bamboo shoots out first and place in the bottom of a heated deep serving dish. Arrange the pieces of chicken on top. Strain the liquid from the pan and add the optional monosodium glutamate and sesame oil. Bring to a boil and pour over the chicken before serving.

Hundred Flower Chicken

PAI HUA CH'I-FANG CHI

1 2-lb. chicken or chicken pieces
2 tbs. fatback
1 cup cooked shelled shrimp (about ⅓ lb.)
1 celery stalk
2 water chestnuts
1 duck egg
1½ tsps. salt
½ tsp. monosodium glutamate (optional)
⅔ cup superior broth
1 tsp. sesame oil
2 tsps. cornstarch
1 tb. water
1 small red sweet pepper
3 scallions
3 leeks

Red-braised Chicken

HUNG TAN TSAOW CHI

1 3-lb. chicken or chicken pieces
¾ cup bamboo shoots
2 scallions
3 tbs. lard
2 tsps. chopped fresh ginger root
3 tbs. wine-sediment paste
1 tb. sugar
3 tbs. light soy sauce
3 tbs. dry sherry
1 cup chicken bouillon
1 tsp. monosodium glutamate (optional)
2 tsps. sesame oil

Drunken Chops

TSUI P'AI KU

4 pork chops
1½ tsp. salt
⅓ cup dry sherry
¼ cup cornstarch
3 water chestnuts
6 tbs. lard
2 cloves garlic
1 tb. chopped scallion
1 tsp. curry powder
1 tb. tangerine (or orange) juice
1 tb. tomato paste
2 tbs. soy sauce
2 tsps. sugar
1 tsp. sesame oil

Deep-fried Fish in Wine-Sediment Paste

CHA TSAO YÜ KUAI

2 lbs. fresh fish (haddock, cod, halibut, or bass)
1 tsp. salt
¼ cup dry sherry
¼ cup wine-sediment paste
2 scallions
vegetable oil for deep-frying
1 tb. lard
1 tb. chopped fresh ginger root
1 tb. chopped onion
1 tsp. sugar
1 tsp. soy sauce
3 tbs. chicken bouillon or superior broth
½ tsp. monosodium glutamate (optional)

Like the Cantonese, the Fukienese have a tendency to incorporate fruit and fish into their meat dishes. The use of tangerine juice here is a typical example.

Cut each pork chop through the bone into 4 pieces. Rub the pieces with the salt and half the sherry and let stand for 30 minutes. Dredge with the cornstarch. Cut each water chestnut into 4 thin slices. Melt the lard in a skillet. Then add the pork and sauté for 6 to 10 minutes, turning the pieces over to ensure that they are evenly fried and cooked through. Drain the pork on paper towels and discard all but 1 tablespoon of the fat from the skillet.

Peel and chop the garlic and add it, along with the scallions and curry powder, to the hot fat in the skillet; then stir-fry for 30 seconds. Add the remaining sherry, the water chestnuts, tangerine juice, tomato paste, soy sauce, and sugar. Continue to stir-fry for another 30 seconds. Add the pork pieces and the sesame oil. Stir-fry gently for 1 minute. Transfer to a heated dish and serve.

❦

This dish is suitable for eating with rice or just to nibble with a drink. The Restaurant of the Gallant Heart, from which this recipe comes, is situated beside the Hung Shan Bridge. As you drink and nibble you can watch the boats shooting down the rapids.

Cut the fish into thick pieces, 2 inches by 1 inch by 1½ inches. Rub with the salt and marinate in a mixture of half the sherry and half the wine-sediment paste for 1 hour. Cut the scallions into 1½-inch segments.

Heat the vegetable oil until very hot and deep-fry the fish in it for 3 to 4 minutes. Drain on paper towels for 1 minute. Then arrange the chunks of fish on a large flat plate.

Heat the lard in a small skillet. Add the ginger and onion and sauté over high heat for 1 minute. Add the remaining sherry, remaining wine-sediment paste, sugar, soy sauce, chicken bouillon or superior broth, and optional monosodium glutamate. Continue to stir-fry for 30 seconds. Pour the sauce over the fish and garnish with the scallions.

Fukien

This dish is unusual in that it needs no real cooking—the sliced kidneys are merely blanched in boiling water.

Remove the skin and discard the core from the kidneys. Cut each one in half and cut again into paper-thin slices. Place in a bowl and marinate for 30 minutes in half the salt and the sherry.

Mix together the remaining salt, sesame jam, sugar, optional monosodium glutamate, and water. Place the sliced kidneys in a large bowl and cover with boiling water. Use a pair of chopsticks to separate the slices. After 30 seconds, drain and cover again with fresh boiling water. By this time the slices of kidney will curl up and should be just cooked.

Arrange the lettuce leaves on a large round serving plate. Place the sliced kidney on top of the lettuce leaves and then pour the sesame jam mixture evenly over the kidney slices. Use prepared mustard as a dip.

Pork Kidneys in Sesame Jam

MA CHIENG YAO PIEN

4 pork kidneys
2 tsps. salt
3 tbs. dry sherry
2 tbs. sesame jam
1 tsp. sugar
½ tsp. monosodium glutamate (optional)
3 tbs. water
1 head of lettuce

Clear-steamed Fish

CHING CHEN YU

1 2–3 lb. fresh fish (gray mullet, bass, or carp)
1½ tsps. salt
2 tsps. sesame oil
1 tsp. monosodium glutamate (optional)
1 slice lean pork
2 tsps. chopped fresh ginger root
3 tbs. soy sauce
2 tsps. sugar
4 scallions
1 tb. lard
4–6 dried Chinese mushrooms, soaked and drained
3 tbs. superior broth
3 tbs. dry sherry
1 tsp. cornstarch

Pork Scallops

TSA LI JOU

2 lbs. pork, fresh shoulder or loin roast
3 tbs. soy sauce
3 tbs. dry sherry
2 bay leaves
1 tb. brown rock sugar
2 medium carrots
6 radishes
2 tsps. salt
1 tb. sugar
1 tb. vinegar
1 tsp. sesame oil
2 duck eggs
1 cup bread crumbs
vegetable oil for deep-frying

The Chinese concept of a good fish dish is like the Western concept of a roast—something informal which may be cut up at the table.

Clean the fish. Rub the inside with a mixture of the salt, sesame oil, and half the optional monosodium glutamate. Cut the pork into matchstick-thin strips. Add the ginger, half the soy sauce, and sugar to the pork. Chop each of the scallions, using stems only, add to the mixture, and set aside. Chop each of the remaining 2 scallion stems into 4 to 6 segments. Put these in a large oval ovenproof dish. Place the fish on top and put the dish in a steamer. Cover and steam (20 minutes for a 2-lb. fish, 30 minutes for 3 lbs.).

Heat the lard in a skillet. Slice the mushrooms and sauté for 5 seconds. Add the pork mixture and stir-fry over high heat. Blend the remaining soy sauce, optional monosodium glutamate, the broth, sherry, and cornstarch. Add the mixture to the skillet. Season to taste. Stir-fry and then pour the mixture over the fish and serve immediately.

There is a well-known Fukien banquet called the "Whole Pig Feast," in which a pig is slaughtered especially for the feast and made into 108 dishes. This is one of them.

Boil the pork in water to cover for 5 minutes. Drain and cut into thin slices. Place the pork in an ovenproof bowl and add the soy sauce, sherry, bay leaves, and rock sugar. Marinate for 30 minutes. Place the bowl of marinated pork in a steamer. Cover and steam for 1 hour. Remove and cool.

Meanwhile, grate the carrots and radishes into a colander, rub the salt into them, and let stand for 10 minutes. Rinse them under cold water, drain, and dry. Put them in a bowl and add the sugar, vinegar, and sesame oil.

When the pork is quite cold and solid, break the eggs into a bowl, beat them lightly, and dip each piece of pork in the egg. Roll the pieces of pork in the bread crumbs until completely covered. Heat the vegetable oil and deep-fry the pork (6 pieces at a time) for 3 minutes, or until golden. Cut each slice of pork into 3 pieces.

Arrange the pieces of bread-crumbed pork around a mound of grated radishes and carrots in the middle of a platter. The pork is crisp, tender, and extremely tasty.

The attractiveness of this dish lies in its color and in the appealing aroma of sherry applied at the last moment.

Beat the egg whites for 2 minutes, or until nearly stiff. Fold in the yolks, salt, and optional monosodium glutamate. Finely chop the pork and scallions. Slice the mushrooms and bamboo shoots into matchstick-thin strips. Place the pork, scallions, mushrooms, bamboo shoots, sugar, soy sauce, and five-spice powder in a bowl. Mix well.

Heat 1 tablespoon of the lard in a small pan. Add the pork mixture and stir-fry for 3 minutes. Remove from the heat and set aside. Melt half the remaining lard in a large skillet over very low heat. Add half the egg mixture, which will spread into a 6-inch circle. When the egg has somewhat set, gently put the cooked pork mixture into the center,

After 1 minute of cooking over low heat, pour the remaining egg mixture over the filling. Heat the remaining lard in a small saucepan until very hot and pour it over the soft egg mixture. Sprinkle the parsley over the omelet; then pour over the sherry. Cook for 30 seconds without stirring. Gently lift one side of the omelet to drain away the lard. Use a spatula to lift the omelet onto a heated serving plate.

Pine-Flower Omelet

SUNG HUA JOU

6 eggs, separated
1 tsp. salt
1 tsp. monosodium glutamate (optional)
¼ lb. lean pork
2 scallions
1 cup dried Chinese mushrooms, soaked and drained
¼ cup bamboo shoots
1 tsp. sugar
1 tb. soy sauce
¼ tsp. five-spice powder
6 tbs. lard
3 tbs. minced parsley
1 tb. dry sherry

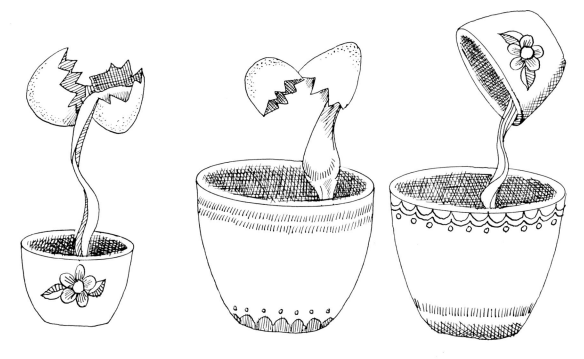

Use three bowls to separate eggs. Crack over the first, letting the white flow into it; put the yolk in the second; and, making sure it contains no yolk, transfer the white to the third. Thus only 1 white will be spoiled if you slip.

Anchovy Pork

YEN YÜ TUN CHU JOU

2 lbs. pork, fresh shoulder or loin
   roast
3 tbs. chopped onion
4 slices fresh ginger root
1 tsp. salt
1¼ cups water
6–12 anchovy fillets, according
   to taste

> In order to maintain an even temperature, use boiling water to replenish the water that evaporates during steaming. Be sure that the level of water never reaches more than halfway up the sides of the casserole.

Bamboo Shoots in Chicken Cream

CHI YUNG CHING CHU SSU

6 cups bamboo shoots in 1½-
   to 2-inch lengths
1 chicken breast
3 tbs. fatback
6 eggs
1 tb. cornstarch
1 tsp. salt
½ tsp. monosodium glutamate
   (optional)
3 sprigs fresh parsley
1¼ cups chicken bouillon
2 tbs. lard
1 tb. chopped cooked ham

The flavor of fresh meat or vegetables is often enhanced by cooking with dried or pickled food. In this recipe, fresh pork is cooked with salted fish, giving it a unique flavor.

Plunge the pork into boiling water to cover and simmer for 10 minutes. Drain and slice the pork across the meat, fat, and skin, so each piece measures about 2 inches long by 1 inch wide by ½-inch thick and has skin attached. Arrange the pork, skinside down, in a casserole. Place the onion, ginger, and salt in a small saucepan, add the water, bring to a boil, and simmer for 5 minutes. Remove from the heat and pour the contents of the pan over the pork. Arrange the anchovy fillets on top of the pork.

Place the casserole in a large saucepan filled with 1 to 1½ inches water. It is essential that the water should not reach more than halfway up the sides of the casserole. Bring the water to a boil, cover, and simmer over a minimum heat for 1½ hours (adding water to the saucepan when necessary). Alternatively, the pork may be steamed for 1¼ hours. After this fairly long cooking period, the taste and saltiness of the anchovy fillets will have penetrated the pork, including the skin, which should be almost jellylike in consistency.

This is a dainty dish for those who do not have a large appetite or for drinkers who only wish to nibble between sips.

With a very sharp knife, cut the bamboo shoots lengthwise into the thinnest possible slices. Then cut the slices into fine strips (about half the thickness of matchsticks). Grind the chicken flesh and fatback twice. Beat the eggs in a bowl. Add the cornstarch, salt, and optional monosodium glutamate and beat to an even consistency. Wash the parsley, separate into small sprigs, and discard the coarser stems.

Place the bamboo shoots in a saucepan. Add the chicken bouillon and simmer for 25 to 30 minutes, or until practically dry. Meanwhile, mix the chicken and fatback with the egg mixture. Heat the lard in a skillet. Add the bamboo shoots and stir-fry for 2 minutes. Add the chicken mixture and stir-fry gently for 2½ minutes. Transfer to a heated serving plate and garnish with the sprigs of parsley and the chopped ham. The crunchiness of the bamboo shoots adds a new dimension to the scrambled eggs, which are made savory by the monosodium glutamate and chicken, smooth by the lard, and colorful by the ham and parsley.

Southwest China

This region of China has sometimes been referred to as the Great Southwest. Although it is a much smaller region than either the Northeast (Manchuria) or the Northwest (Sinkiang), it is composed of three provinces: Yunnan, Kweichow, and Kwangsi—portions of all three being within the tropics. The area totals approximately two-hundred-seventy thousand square miles and has a population of thirty-five million.

Isolated from the mainstream of events during the past half-century, it was in a way rediscovered by the people of the East Coast during the War of Resistance against Japan, when a great number of enterprises, government offices, and educational institutions had to move westward. The communication between the East Coast and this area was so poor that those who moved to these back provinces of China had to travel hundreds of miles on foot, or else go by sea to Haiphong and Hanoi and come back into China again via the Hanoi-Yunnanfu railroad.

The Great Southwest is the one area in China where the mountain ranges and rivers run north-south, rather than east-west. Among the great rivers of the region is the Mekong, called in Chinese the Gold Sand River. Much of China's rich output of tin comes from these provinces.

Until recently, it was a feudal area, in spite of more than thirty years of the Chinese Republican rule. The lords and ladies (rather, the warlords and their concubines) ate very well; their tables, like Henry VIII's high table, offered *haute cuisine* of sorts. The cooking of this area originates from these feudal "high tables" and uses a wide choice of local produce.

The tropical and subtropical portions of the provinces produce a wide variety of fruit: oranges, bananas, pomelos, papaws, pineapple, and lichees. From the inland lakes of Tien and Erhhai, five thousand feet above sea level, come many types of freshwater fish. Carp, cod, haddock, bass, halibut, mullet—all contribute to the great variety of dishes.

Geographically, the region is beautiful. In Kwangsi, there are numerous hills and mountains that rise perpendicularly, like stalagmites. Despite a mild climate and adequate rainfall, there is not much agriculture because the soil is scanty and poor. Its chief crops are rice, corn, wheat, and tea.

Yunnan, which borders on Burma and Indochina, is largely a region of high plateaus separated by unnavigable rivers flowing through deep gorges. Livestock is raised on the steep slopes, and from the meager land that's left for cultivation come good harvests of wheat, rice, fruits, and tobacco. Transportation is poor, and although the area is rich in minerals, it remains unexploited because of its inaccessibility. Kunming, the capital of Yunnan, has the reputation of enjoying the best weather in China.

The ham from Yunnan is one of the best known in the country. The meat is uniquely sweet and mild. The province also produces an excellent goat's cheese (although the Chinese diet is very spare in dairy products).

The soup-snack dish, which seems to be a Yunnan specialty, would hardly be considered a snack according to Western standards. With a hot bowl of broth in front of you, you help yourself to small paper-thin strips of meat, chicken, and/or fish which you dip into the broth and eat. Small pieces of vegetables are then dipped and eaten. By now, the broth has taken on all the flavors of the meats, fish, and vegetables, and you simply add noodles that have been semicooked, along with whatever vegetables are left.

Incidentally, the powerful tonic tea called *Po Nay Chaah*—a red brick variety—comes from the province of Yunnan, as do some of China's best black teas.

In Kweichow, the most mountainous, and the nearest of the three to the Central Provinces, the cooking is motivated by the mid-Yangtze and the Szechwan cuisine. Since it is an extremely poor area, its cuisine is largely composed of its own home-cooking style and these outside influences.

Kweichow is renowned for the salt-and-sour pickle made there. (See Glossary for two do-it-yourself versions.) The flavor is quite distinctive and lends itself well to fish and pork dishes. Two such dishes are *Yen Suan Yu* (fish) and *Yen Suan K'ou J'ou* (pork).

Kwangsi, although fiercely independent, is much like its twin province, Kwangtung, in climate, natural resources, and agriculture. Kwangtung, however, is richer and more heavily populated (and is the originator of the varied Cantonese cuisine).

In these back provinces of China, much of the local produce and distinctive ingredients are uncommon plants and animals rarely seen or heard of anywhere else. Bear's paws and sparrows are quite common delicacies. In the selection of recipes here, we have confined ourselves to dishes whose ingredients are generally available in Western kitchens.

Velvet of Chicken in Bean-Flower Soup

CHI YUNG TOU HUA

2 oz. chicken breast
2 oz. fatback
2 oz. fish fillet (carp, cod, haddock, bass, or halibut)
3 egg whites
1 tb. chopped onion
1½ tsps. chopped fresh ginger root
⅓ cup superior broth
1 tsp. salt
⅔ cup bean or green pea soup
1 tsp. sesame oil

Fry-braised Fish Balls

CH'AO HUA YÜ KU

2 lbs. fresh fish (carp, cod, haddock, bass, or halibut)
1 egg
1½ tsps. salt
½ tsp. monosodium glutamate (optional)
2 tsps. sesame oil
3 tbs. water
½ small green sweet pepper
3 water chestnuts
8 dried Chinese mushrooms, soaked and drained
2 cloves garlic
vegetable oil for deep-frying
¼ cup vegetable oil
⅓ cup bean sprouts
3 slices fresh ginger root
1 tb. chutney
¼ cup superior broth
2 tbs. cornstarch

There are many dishes in Chinese cooking that may appear somewhat mushy to Westerners, but they have a special function in the procession of dishes in a multicourse Chinese dinner. This is one of them—a Yunnan speciality.

Simmer the chicken, fatback, and fish in water to cover for 15 minutes. Drain and grind finely. Add the egg whites and beat 20 strokes. Boil the onion and ginger in the broth for 5 minutes. Add the salt and pepper to taste. Strain the broth into the chicken mixture and mix well. Bring the bean soup to a boil. Pour half into the chicken mixture and set the remainder aside.

Stir the chicken mixture well. Place the bowl in a steamer, cover, and steam for 20 minutes. Pour the mixture into a soup tureen. Heat the remaining soup and pour it on top. Sprinkle with the sesame oil before serving.

This dish is very popular in Kwangsi homes. It is a recipe used by many well-known chefs in Nanting.

Clean the fish, fillet it, and grind the flesh. Beat the egg and add it to the fish together with 1 teaspoon of the salt, the optional monosodium glutamate, half the sesame oil, pepper to taste, and the water. Beat well. Form into balls about ½ inch in diameter. Thinly slice the green pepper and water chestnuts. Remove and discard the mushroom stems. Peel and slice the garlic.

Deep-fry the fish balls in the hot oil for 2 minutes. Drain and simmer in boiling water for 2 minutes. Drain again and set aside.

Place the ¼ cup oil in a large skillet. Place over high heat for 30 seconds. Add the remaining salt, the green pepper, water chestnuts, mushrooms, garlic, bean sprouts, ginger, and chutney. Stir-fry quickly for 2 minutes. Add the fish balls and continue to stir-fry over lower heat for 1 minute. Add the broth and cornstarch blended with a little water. Stir for 10 seconds and sprinkle with the remaining sesame oil. Serve immediately.

Honeyed-Pear Ham

MI LA HUO T'UI

½ lb. Yunnan ham or cooked
  smoked ham, sliced
3 medium pears, fresh or canned
vegetable oil for deep-frying
¾ cup brown rock sugar
3 tbs. cornstarch
½ cup water

> Pour boiling water over canned
> pears to remove excess sweet-
> ness if fresh or water-packed
> pears are not available.

Yunnan ham is one of the best-known hams in China. It has a mild, sweet taste. The Yunnanese like saltiness combined with sweetness, as in this recipe.

Cut the ham slices into pieces, 2 inches long by 1 inch wide. Place these in a bowl. If using fresh pears, peel and core them, cut into eighths, and deep-fry for 20 seconds in hot oil. Then place them on top of the ham. If using canned pears, do not add at this stage.

Sprinkle the fresh pears and ham (or ham only) with a third of the rock sugar and steam for 25 minutes. If canned pears are used, drain them well, cut into eighths, and add to the steamer after 15 minutes. Blend the remaining sugar and cornstarch with the water in a saucepan. Mix well. Bring to a boil, stirring until thick. Arrange the pears and ham on a large heated serving dish and pour the sauce over them.

Salt-and-Sour Fish

YEN SUAN YÜ

1 2–3 lb. fresh fish (carp, bass, or
  mullet)
1 tsp. salt
⅓ cup Kweichow salt-and-sour
  pickle
1 clove garlic
1 medium onion
3 slices fresh ginger root
1 tb. soy sauce
1 tb. dry sherry
2 tsps. sugar
2 tbs. lard
1¼ cups water
1 tsp. monosodium glutamate
  (optional)
1½ tsps. sesame oil
1 tb. cornstarch

Chinese sweet-and-sour dishes are quite well known in the West, but it is not often that one comes upon a salt-and-sour dish. It is a taste developed by the cooks of Kweichow, and fish cooked in this manner is said to have a recognizable Kweichow flavor.

Clean the fish, rub with the salt, both inside and out, and let stand for 1 hour. Chop the salt-and-sour pickle, garlic, and onion and combine them with the ginger, soy sauce, sherry, and sugar.

Heat the lard in a kettle. Add the salt and sour mixture and stir-fry over high heat for 30 seconds. Add the water and bring to a boil, stirring constantly.

Lower the fish into the boiling sauce and simmer for 10 minutes, turning the fish over once and basting all the time. Carefully lift the fish onto an oval heated serving dish. Add pepper, optional monosodium glutamate, and sesame oil to the sauce. Pour in the cornstarch blended with a little water. Stir and, as soon as the sauce thickens, pour it over the fish and serve.

This dish derived its name from its resemblance to the Chinese New Year cannon-cracker (fire-cracker).

Cut the chicken flesh into small thin slices. Cut the pork into thin slices about 3 inches by 2 inches. Lay the slices of pork on a large plate or tray. Brush them with the soy sauce and sprinkle with the salt, sugar, onion, and ginger. Lay a piece of chicken on top of each piece of pork. Cut the ham into strips and place a strip in the center of each piece of chicken. Roll up, wrapping the ham and chicken inside. Tie each roll securely with 2 of the chives (if unavailable, secure with a wooden toothpick).

Beat the eggs and mix with the cornstarch to make a thin batter. Dip each pork-chicken roll lightly into the batter. Deep-fry the rolls in hot oil for 5 to 6 minutes. Drain. remove the toothpicks if used, and arrange on a heated dish. Sprinkle with the sesame oil and serve.

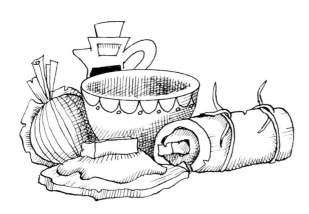

Though boiled, fried, and then steamed, the name of this dish comes from the method of serving.

Boil the pork in water to cover for 7 to 8 minutes. Drain and deep-fry it in the hot oil for 7 to 8 minutes. Drain again and, with a sharp knife, cut into pieces 2¼-inches long by 1¼ inches wide by ½ inch thick. Arrange the pieces of pork, skinside down, in an ovenproof dish. Place the ginger in a bowl and add the soy sauce and sherry. Pour the ginger mixture evenly over the pork. Add the salt-and-sour pickle. Place in a steamer, cover, and steam for 1 to 1¼ hours.

This dish should be brought to the table and tipped out onto a large deep serving dish or tureen, so that the pork will have its skinside up. It should be eaten with a large quantity of rice.

Cannon- Cracker Chicken

PAO CHU CHI

1 chicken breast
½ lb. pork shoulder (fat part without skin)
1 tb. soy sauce
½ tsp. salt
1½ tsps. sugar
1 tb. chopped onion
1½ tsps. chopped fresh ginger root
2 slices cooked smoked ham
1 bunch chives
2 eggs
1 tb. cornstarch
vegetable oil for deep-frying
1 tsp. sesame oil

Salt-and-Sour Tip-Out Pork

YEN SUAN K'OU JOU

2 lbs. pork, fresh picnic shoulder or loin roast, with skin
vegetable oil for deep-frying
3 tsps. chopped fresh ginger root
1 tb. soy sauce
2 tbs. sweet sherry
⅓ cup Kweichow salt-and-sour pickle

The Yunnan Snack

KUO' CH'IAO MI CHIEN

6 cups duck or chicken broth
½ tsp. salt
¼ tsp. monosodium glutamate
  (optional)
¼ lb. chicken breast
¼ lb. pork tenderloin
¼ lb. fresh fish (sole, bass,
  salmon, carp, or haddock)
¼ lb. pork liver
¼ lb. pork kidney
3 cups Chinese celery cabbage
¼ lb. spinach
1⅓ cups bean sprouts
1 cup egg noodles (or rice
  noodles)

FOR THE DIPS:
soy sauce
vinegar
Haisein sauce
sesame oil
salt
pepper

This tea-house food is usually prepared for one customer at a time. However, quantities given here are sufficient for four. The diner dips thinly sliced raw meat in the hot broth for several minutes. After eating the meat, he dips parboiled vegetables and, finally, semicooked noodles. By this time the broth will be cooler, tastier, and suitable for drinking.

The broth should be prepared beforehand by prolonged simmering (5 to 6 hours) of a duck or chicken carcass. By the time it is ready to be served, at least 2 tablespoons duck or chicken fat should be left in the broth, which will help it to retain heat at the table. Add the salt, optional monosodium glutamate, and pepper to taste. Slice the chicken, pork, and fish in paper-thin strips about 2 inches by 1 inch. Dip the liver and kidney in boiling water for 1 minute and drain. Slice into paper-thin strips. Arrange the meats and fish on a small dish.

Cut the vegetables into pieces 1-inch long. Plunge them, one vegetable at a time, into boiling water for 1 minute and cool in fresh water for 3 minutes. Drain and arrange by color on a separate dish. Boil the noodles for 5 to 6 minutes, drain, and place on a third dish.

Heat one-half of the broth to boiling and place it in a tureen or ovenproof casserole that will hold the heat. Bring the hot broth to the table and reserve the rest. The diner eats the meats first. Using chopsticks, he submerges the pieces which require longer heating. The pieces which require less cooking he merely dips into the soup for 1 minute or so. The meats are usually eaten in a leisurely fashion, after dipping each piece in one or two dips. After the meats have been eaten, the different vegetables are added to the broth, along with the reserved broth, which should be freshly boiled. After half the vegetables have been consumed in the same fashion as the meats, the noodles are poured into the broth. From then on, the multidish snack becomes a noodle soup, which is not just a soup but a meal.

Pot-steamed Chicken

CH'I KUO CHI

1 3–4 lb. chicken
2 slices fresh ginger root
2 tsps. salt
1 tsp. monosodium glutamate
   (optional)

After chopping the chicken (see page 55 for a note on how this is done), carefully inspect the pieces for bone splinters and remove any that you find.

This Yunnan dish is well-known throughout China, and the method of cooking—steaming—is considered the purest way to prepare food.

Clean the chicken and chop (including bones) into about 24 pieces. Place the neck and bonier parts of the chicken around the bottom of a casserole or steam pot. Build up layers, piece by piece, with the meatier portions until you reach the top layer, which should be slices of the chicken breast. Place the ginger slices over the chicken. Sprinkle with half the salt and put on the lid. Cover and steam for about 3 hours.

When the steaming is complete, remove the lid and sprinkle the chicken with the remaining salt, pepper to taste, and the optional monosodium glutamate. The steam pot, which is often a decorative piece of pottery, should be brought to the table and the lid opened ceremoniously in front of the diners.

These spinach balls have a heart of meat.

Beat the eggs for 1 minute and then mix well into the pork. Boil the ginger, onion, and water in a saucepan. Remove from the heat and let stand for 6 minutes. Strain, discard the ginger and onion, and pour the water into the pork mixture. Add the cornstarch, half the optional monosodium glutamate, half the salt, and pepper to taste. Beat the mixture for 1 minute. Form into small meatballs.

Wash the spinach, remove the stems, and add to a large pan of boiling water for a 10-second dip. Drain well and slice into matchstick-thin strips. Slice the mushrooms, bamboo shoots, and ham into similar-sized strips. Mix together and spread on a tray. Roll the meatballs over this to pick up the various colored strips. Place them on an ovenproof plate. Cover and steam for 8 minutes.

Arrange the remaining spinach, mushrooms, bamboo shoots, and ham in the bottom of a heated deep ovenproof dish. Place the meatballs on top. Meanwhile, make a sauce with the broth by adding the remaining optional monosodium glutamate, remaining salt, and pepper to taste. Heat and pour over the meatballs. Sprinkle with sesame oil.

Spinach Balls

PO T'SAI YUAN TZU

¼ lb. fat fresh pork ground and mixed with ½ lb. lean fresh pork
3 eggs
1 tsp. chopped fresh ginger root
2 tbs. chopped onion
½ cup water
1 tb. cornstarch
½ tsp. monosodium glutamate (optional)
1 tsp. salt
2 lbs. spinach
1 cup dried Chinese mushrooms, soaked and drained
½ cup bamboo shoots
2 tbs. cooked smoked ham
1¼ cups superior broth
1 tsp. sesame oil

Canton

Among Westerners, Cantonese cuisine is the most popular of all regional styles of cooking. Egg roll, roast pork, egg foo yung—all originated in the kitchens of Canton. Of all the regional schools and the enormous range of Chinese cooking, the Cantonese style of the province of Kwangtung has the widest variety of dishes. It includes the largest collection of regional dishes in the whole of China; and, excluding the French, it has probably the largest repertoire of dishes in the world.

To a large extent, food and cuisine must necessarily be the product of the geography of that region. Geographically, Kwangtung is the Louisiana of China and Canton, her capital, is her New Orleans. Canton, however, is a more important city industrially, and Kwangtung is much larger and more heavily populated than Louisiana. It has a population of thirty-eight million, and a coastline that zigzags for nearly a thousand miles. Its principal cities and towns are situated along the Pearl River and its tributaries, the West River and the smaller East River.

It was from here that the main bulk of Chinese emigrants went abroad to develop and enrich themselves in the South Seas. In the nineteenth century, several tens of thousands of them crossed the Pacific to San Francisco, where they founded the famous Chinatown and helped to build the Union Pacific.

According to legend, it was during the building of the railway that chop suey was born. The hard-working Chinese coolies simply could not accustom themselves to American food and cooking; they needed their rice foods. In desperation, the American railway people threw up their hands and turned the cooking over to the laborers themselves. The result was a massive, makeshift stew of little bits of pork combined with whatever vegetables were available, and the concoction was spooned over a bowl of rice.

Later, some of these self-made cooks went into business for themselves and opened their own chop suey houses, selling the simple but filling dish to their fellow Chinese. In time, the very low cost and not unpleasant taste of this dish began to appeal to Americans. As the little Chinese restaurant began to find its way across the country, the quality of the dish improved—and Chinese cooking generally became more varied and sophisticated.

Canton—once the Gate to China—is not just a port, but thousands of ports. The sea and three rivers converge here to make it the "water city" and the Cantonese "those who live on the water." Wherever you look, there are boats and people living on them, in sampans, junks, and rafts. There are floating restaurants, hotels, libraries, hospitals, and nursery schools.

The climate of Kwangtung is temperate year-round, verging on the semitropical, and fresh food is always available. Fruit grows in abundance: green bananas, figs, pineapples, the sweet lichee, oranges, and lemons. The gardeners of the province raise hundreds of different kinds of tea plants, and camellias grow in profusion.

Among the great teas that come from Kwangtung are the green tea called "Water Nymph," the blackish-red "Black Dragon Tea," and the red tea known as "Clear Distance."

The long coastline produces a constant supply of seafood, which is a specialty of the region. The Cantonese boast that their shark's-fin soup is the best in China. Oysters from the sea, eel, snakes, and snails are cleverly combined in the cuisine, along with the frogs and turtles found in the watery rice fields. The Cantonese are fond of mixing meat with the taste of seafood.

Classically featured at the simplest tables, as well as the grandest, are all sorts of birds: sparrows (fried), pigeons, wild ducks, and chicken. The Cantonese are especially ingenious and artful in chicken cuisine. They are also masters with mushroom, which Nature supplies generously here, along with many leafy vegetables and greens. (Some Chinese believe that you should not talk while eating mushrooms because it spoils the flavor of the fungus.)

Roasted meats, especially pork, are traditional to the region, as are steamed dishes of all sorts. Southern cooking is the least greasy of all the regional styles. The emphasis is on fast cooking, mostly stir-frying, which brings the food to the peak of its natural color, and they use a lighter-colored soy sauce, so as not to detract from the naturalness of the color.

The Cantonese recipes in this book were derived from restaurants and eating houses actually situated in the area. Care was taken to omit those recipes that are obviously unacceptable (those using snakes and wild cats, for example!), or whose ingredients are difficult to come by.

Won Ton Soup with Bamboo Shoots

MU ERH HUN TUN T'ANG

FOR THE *Hun Tun* SKIN:
1½ cups all-purpose flour
⅓ cup water
½ tsp. lard

FOR THE FILLING:
1 tsp. sesame oil
½ small onion, chopped
2 water chestnuts, chopped
¼ cup finely ground fresh pork

FOR THE SOUP:
1½ cups wood-ears, soaked for 1
    hour, or button mushrooms
½ cup cabbage heart
3 tbs. chopped leeks
2 slices fresh ginger root
1¼ cups water
3¾ cups superior broth
2 tbs. soy sauce
⅓ cup bamboo shoots
½ tsp. sesame oil
1 tsp. monosodium glutamate
    (optional)
vegetable oil for deep-frying

Very thin-skinned fried won tons, made from Hun Tun *skin, are used in this soup, as croutons are used in Western soups. Wood-ears are used for texture rather than taste.*

To make the *Hun Tun* skin, add a pinch of salt to the water and bring it to a boil. Sift the flour into a bowl, add the boiling water, and stir quickly with a wooden spoon. Add the lard and knead well on a floured board. After kneading, roll the dough into a very thin sheet about 24 inches by 16 inches. Cut the sheet into 24 3½- to 4-inch squares.

For the filling, mix together the onion, water chestnuts, and pork. Heat the sesame oil in a small skillet and saute the filling mixture for 2 minutes. Remove from the heat and cool. Divide the filling into 24 portions and wrap each portion in a *Hun Tun* skin. Set the filled won tons aside.

For the soup, boil the wood-ears along with the cabbage in water to cover for 5 minutes. Discard the water. Boil the leeks and ginger in the 1¼ cups water for 10 minutes. Add the wood-ears, cabbage, 1¼ cups of the superior broth, the soy sauce, and bamboo shoots to the leeks and ginger. Simmer for 10 minutes.

Pour this soup into a large ovenproof tureen. Add the sesame oil, remaining superior broth, the optional monosodium glutamate, and salt and pepper to taste. Steam or simmer slowly for an additional 15 minutes.

While the soup is simmering, deep-fry the filled won tons in hot oil for about 4 minutes, or until golden. Place the fried won tons at the bottom of a large, heated tureen and pour the soup over them. Serve immediately, while the crackling won tons are "singing" in the tureen.

Cream of Chinese Cabbage Soup

NAI YU PAI T'SAI T'ANG

1 lb. Chinese celery cabbage
2½ cups superior broth
1 tsp. salt
1¼ cups milk
1 tb. lard
1 tsp. monosodium glutamate
  (optional)
1 tb. cornstarch
3 tbs. water

The use of milk in this recipe is a sign of Western influence, which is occasionally noticeable in Cantonese cooking.

Cut the cabbage into pieces, 1 inch by ½ inch. Wash thoroughly. Heat the broth. Add the cabbage and simmer for 15 minutes. Then add the salt, milk, lard, optional monosodium glutamate, and pepper. Bring to a boil. Add the cornstarch blended with the water and simmer for an additional 5 minutes. Serve in a heated tureen.

Cantonese Chicken, Ham, and Liver

KUANGCHOW WEN-CHANG CHI

¾ lb. sliced cooked smoked ham
1 medium head cabbage (about
  1½ lbs.)
2½ cups superior broth
1 3-lb. chicken, or chicken
  pieces
¼ lb. chicken livers
2 cups secondary broth
1 tsp. salt
1 tsp. sugar
½ tsp. monosodium glutamate
  (optional)
1 tb. cornstarch
1 tb. water
1 tsp. lard

This is an extremely attractive dish with the contrasting colors and textures of the three meats and the green vegetables.

Cut the ham into 24 thin pieces, 2 inches by 1 inch. Remove and discard the outer leaves of the cabbage, leaving only the hearts and tender leaves. Wash these and cut them into 18 pieces.

Bring the superior broth to a boil in a saucepan. Lower the chicken and livers into it. When the broth reboils, remove from the heat and cool for 30 minutes.

Take the chicken out of the broth, cut the meat from the bone, and slice it into 24 slices. Cut the livers similarly. Reserve the broth. Cook the cabbage in boiling water for 5 minutes. Drain, add the secondary broth and three-quarters of the salt. Boil for another 5 minutes.

Arrange the ham, chicken, and livers in 3 rows down the middle of an oval serving plate. Arrange the cabbage around the meats. Place the plate in a steamer and steam for 5 minutes.

Meanwhile, make a sauce by measuring ¼ cup of the reserved superior broth into a pan. Add the sugar, remaining salt, the optional monosodium glutamate, the cornstarch blended with the water, and the lard. Heat for 1 minute. Remove the plate from the steamer. Pour the sauce over the chicken before serving.

Usually eaten as a snack, these noodles are placed in the center of the table and divided into equal portions among the diners.

Slice the beef or pork, bamboo shoots, leeks, and mushrooms into matchstick-thin strips. Cut the cabbage into 1-inch pieces.

Heat half the oil in a large skillet and sauté the noodles. After turning them over a few times, press the noodles evenly against the bottom of the skillet with a wooden spoon until they form a flat pancake. Cook over medium heat until the noodles at the bottom have become crispy—about 4 minutes. Turn the noodles over in one toss, like flipping a pancake. Sauté for an additional 3 minutes. Then transfer to a heated plate. Keep warm.

Heat the lard in the skillet. Add the leeks, then the meat strips, and stir-fry for 10 to 15 seconds. Add half the soy sauce and then the bamboo shoots and mushrooms. Sprinkle with pepper. Stir-fry for 1 minute. Then transfer the meat mixture to a plate and set aside.

Sprinkle the cabbage with salt and sauté in the remaining oil over high heat for 1 minute. Return the meat mixture to the skillet with the cabbage and sauté together for an additional 30 seconds.

Meanwhile, blend the cornstarch with the water. Then add the remaining soy sauce, bouillon, white wine, sesame oil, optional monosodium glutamate, and sugar. Mix well and pour into the skillet. After 15 seconds, lift out the meat and cabbage mixture, place over the noodles, and pour the sauce from the skillet evenly over the top.

Cantonese Fried Noodles

KWANGTUNG CHOW MEIN

1½ lbs. lean beef steak or pork
½ cup bamboo shoots
2 leeks
2 cups dried Chinese mushrooms, soaked and drained
¼ lb. Chinese cabbage
¼ cup vegetable oil
1 lb. fine egg noodles, cooked
1 tb. lard
1 tb. soy sauce
1 tb. cornstarch
3 tbs. water
3 tbs. chicken bouillon
1 tb. white wine
1 tsp. sesame oil
¼ tsp. monosodium glutamate (optional)
1 tsp. sugar

If you can't master the art of tossing the noodles slip them onto a plate, cover with another plate, turn, then slip them back into the frying pan.

Crystal Chicken

SHUI CHING LENG KENG CHI

1 2–3 lb. chicken
¼ lb. cooked smoked ham
1 tsp. salt
1 tsp. monosodium glutamate (optional)
¼ cup dry sherry
2 envelopes powdered gelatin
3¾ cups superior broth

To speed the melting of the gelatin, let it soften in the broth for 5 minutes before heating the mixture.

Jellied meat (or meat and fish in aspic) appears frequently in Chinese cooking. This dish is particulary attractive garnished with a colorful fruit or vegetable—strips of red or green sweet peppers or strawberries, for example.

Clean the chicken thoroughly and dry. Place the chicken in a saucepan, cover with water, bring to a boil, and simmer for 1 hour. Drain and, when cool, chop the chicken into 24 pieces. Cut the ham into similar sized pieces. Arrange the pieces of chicken and ham, interlaced in rooftile fashion, in an oval dish.

Add the salt, optional monosodium glutamate, sherry, and gelatin to the broth. Heat the broth mixture, stirring until the gelatin has melted and the ingredients are well mixed. Cool for 15 minutes and then pour over the chicken. Place the dish in the refrigerator for 2 hours. After 2 hours, the jellied chicken and ham should have set. Turn it out on a plate and serve.

Easy to make successfully, this dish looks very professional. The recipe comes from the Ping Hung Shing Restaurant, one of Canton's best.

Soak the shrimp in the salt water in the refrigerator for 2 hours. Drain, rinse quickly, and dry thoroughly. Mix the cornstarch with the egg whites, broth, and salt. Stir the shrimp into this mixture. Heat the lard in a skillet until the fat begins to smoke. Add the shrimp mixture and scramble-fry for 30 to 40 seconds over high heat. Remove the shrimp from the skillet and set aside.

Reheat the skillet and add the garlic, scallions, and ginger. Sauté in the lard remaining in the skillet for 10 seconds. Return the shrimp to the skillet, and stir-fry for 10 seconds. Blend together the cornstarch, optional monosodium glutamate, and water. Add this mixture to the skillet and stir gently until the shrimp take on a glistening, glossy look. Serve immediately with quantities of rice.

Crystal Shrimp

PO LI HSIA JEN

1 lb. cooked, shelled shrimp

2½ cups salt water (use 1 tb. salt)

2 tsps. cornstarch

2 egg whites

3 tbs. superior broth

½ tsp. salt

2 tbs. lard

1 clove garlic, crushed

1 tb. chopped scallion

1½ tsps. chopped fresh ginger root

FOR THE SAUCE MIXTURE:

2 tbs. cornstarch

1 tsp. monosodium glutamate (optional)

¼ cup water

Onion-simmered Duck

TS'UNG YU CHIA HSIANG YA

2 onions
¼ lb. roast fresh pork
4 cups dried Chinese mushrooms,
    soaked and drained
1 tsp. salt
1 tb. vegetable oil
1 2–2½ lb. duck
1 tb. light soy sauce
2 cabbage hearts
vegetable oil for deep-frying
1¼ cups superior broth
½ tsp. monosodium glutamate
    (optional)
1½ tsps. oyster sauce

The richness of the dish is counterbalanced by the cabbage and the quantity of onions used. A large quantity of rice is an excellent accompaniment.

Cut each onion into 6 sections. Slice the roast meat (across meat and fat) into strips 1 inch long by ¼-inch wide. Remove and discard the stems from the soaked mushrooms. Sprinkle the mushroom caps with half the salt and sauté in the oil for 2 minutes. Combine these ingredients to make a stuffing. Rub the skin of the duck with soy sauce and stuff with the mixture. Cut the cabbage hearts vertically through the middle into quarters.

Plunge the duck into very hot oil and deep-fry for 1 minute. Drain. Place the duck in a double boiler. Pour the broth over the duck and add the remaining salt, the optional monosodium glutamate, and oyster sauce. Cook slowly over simmering water for 1 hour. Then lift out the duck and line the pot with the leaves of the cabbage hearts. Replace the duck in the center of the pot and simmer for an additional 30 minutes.

Sliced Steak in Oyster Sauce

HAO YU NIU JOY

½ lb. beef tenderloin
3 tbs. dry sherry
1 tb. soy sauce
1 tb. cornstarch
1 tb. water
⅓ cup vegetable oil
2 tb. oyster sauce
¼ cup superior broth
4–6 scallions
3 slices fresh ginger root

Mingling of sea-taste with meat is typically Cantonese. This is an excellent party dish since it is comparatively easy.

Cut the meat across the grain into thin slices, 1½ inches by 1 inch. Place in a bowl along with half the sherry, the soy sauce, and half the cornstarch blended with the water. Mix thoroughly. Add 1 tablespoon vegetable oil and work it into the meat with your fingers.

In another bowl, mix the remaining cornstarch, the oyster sauce, and broth. Cut the scallions into 1-inch segments, using the white part only. Heat the remaining vegetable oil in a skillet over high heat. When very hot, add the beef. Stir-fry for 30 seconds. Remove the beef and discard all but 1 tablespoon of oil. Replace the skillet over the heat and sauté the scallions and ginger for 20 seconds.

Replace the beef in the skillet and pour in the remaining sherry. Spread the beef evenly in the skillet. Quickly pour in the oyster sauce mixture. Stir-fry for about 10 seconds over high heat and transfer to a heated plate before serving.

Spareribs are very popular in Chinese restaurants in the West. This recipe, with its bold use of fruit juices, is a most unusual one.

Separate each rib and chop across the bone into 1-inch lengths, or leave whole. In a bowl combine the leeks with the salt, sugar, soy sauce, and optional monosodium glutamate. Add the spareribs and marinate for 30 minutes. Dust with cornstarch and mix well.

Heat the oil in a skillet, add the ribs, and stir-fry gently for 25 minutes or until golden. Drain off all but 1 tablespoon of oil and set the ribs aside.

Sauté the onion for 1 minute in the oil remaining in the skillet. Add the spareribs. Pour in the apple juice, orange juice, tomato paste, broth, and sherry. Stir-fry for 1 minute. Cover the skillet and cook for 5 to 6 minutes, or until the liquid has largely evaporated. Serve on a heated dish.

> Leeks are sometimes sandy when purchased, and must then be washed very thoroughly. Split the stalk lengthwise, then separate the layers and rinse each piece in cold running water. When sealed tightly in plastic wrap, leeks will keep up to a week in the refrigerator.

Easy to make and quick to serve, this soup is often served in Cantonese homes.

Finely chop the chicken flesh and mix thoroughly in a bowl with the egg whites. Bring the chicken bouillon to a boil in a pan. Add the corn and then stir in the cornstarch mixed with the water. When the contents reboil, stir in the chicken mixture. Stirring gently, add the peas, salt, and optional monosodium glutamate. Simmer for 5 to 6 minutes over low heat.

Chop the ham finely. Pour the soup into a heated tureen and garnish with the chopped ham.

Spareribs Braised in Fruit Juice

KUO CHIH KUO PAI KU

2 lbs. meaty spareribs
3 tbs. finely chopped leeks
1 tsp. salt
2 tsps. sugar
2 tbs. light soy sauce
½ tsp. monosodium glutamate (optional)
1 tb. cornstarch
¼ cup vegetable oil
3 tbs. chopped onion
1 tb. apple juice
1 tb. orange juice
1 tb. tomato paste
⅓ cup secondary broth
3 tbs. dry sherry

Chicken Velvet and Corn Soup

CHI YUNG SHU MI

1 chicken breast
2 egg whites
3¾ cups chicken bouillon
1 7-oz. can whole kernel corn
1 tb. cornstarch
¼ cup water
3 tbs. fresh green peas
1 tsp. salt
½ tsp. monosodium glutamate (optional)
1 thin slice smoked cooked ham

Sweet and Sour Pork

KU LAO JOU

½ lb. pork, fresh shoulder or loin
1 tsp. salt
1 tb. dry sherry
1 egg
1 tb. cornstarch
1 green or red sweet pepper
1 leek
½ small onion
½ cup bamboo shoots
⅓ cup vegetable oil

FOR THE SWEET AND SOUR SAUCE:
½ cup brown sugar
3 tbs. white vinegar
1 tb. tangerine (or orange) juice
1 tb. tomato paste
1 tb. soy sauce
1 tb. cornstarch

When making this famous dish, it is important to keep the pork crisp and distinctively tasty although immersed in a pronounced sweet-sour sauce. The latter, when well made, is translucent and has a fruity and refreshing taste.

Cut away the skin from the pork. Dice the meat into ½-inch cubes. Add the salt and sherry and marinate for 30 minutes. Make a batter with the egg mixed with the cornstarch. Trim the pepper, remove the seeds, and cut into thin strips. Cut the leek into ½-inch sections. Chop the onion and the bamboo shoots into slices ½ inch by ½ inch by ¼ inch.

For the sauce, mix together the brown sugar, vinegar, tangerine juice, tomato paste, and soy sauce. Heat the mixture in a small pan until the sugar completely dissolves. Remove the pan from the heat.

Coat the pork in the batter. Heat the oil in a skillet. Pour in the pork and stir-fry gently over high heat for 2½ minutes. Add the bamboo shoots and continue to stir-fry for 30 seconds. Remove the pork and bamboo shoots and set aside. Pour off all but 1 tablespoon of oil.

Replace the skillet over the heat and add the pepper, leek, and onion. Stir-fry for 1 minute. Add the cornstarch to the sweet and sour sauce, blend well, and pour it into the skillet. Stir gently until the contents reboil. Then add the partially cooked pork and bamboo shoots. After a few quick stirs and scrambles, transfer to a heated plate and serve.

❧

Another example of the Cantonese use of fruit with meat, this dish is highly palatable.

Steamed Pork Chops with Plums

MEI TZU CHENG P'AI KU

4–5 pork chops
1 tsp. salt
3 tbs. dry white wine
6 plums
4½ tsps. light soy sauce
2 tsps. sugar
1 tb. cornstarch

Cut each chop across the bone into 3 pieces. Rub with salt and marinate in the wine for 30 minutes. Remove the pits from the plums and cut each plum into 3 pieces. Add the plums and the soy sauce to the pork and sprinkle with the sugar. Add the cornstarch and mix the ingredients with your fingers.

Arrange the pieces of pork and plums alternately in neat rows in an ovenproof dish. Place the dish in a steamer. Cover and steam over high heat for 40 to 45 minutes, or until the meat separates easily from the bone. Bring the dish immediately to the table. Dark soy sauce may be used as a dip.

Menu Planning, Tea and Wine Guide

The planning and preparation of authentic Chinese meals can be an exciting and rewarding experience. With time and practice, anyone who enjoys cooking will become proficient at it. Whether you intend to serve a complete Chinese dinner, or only one or two dishes to accompany a Western meal, these wonderfully efficient cooking methods should be learned and utilized.

Your time must be planned carefully, for many of the dishes require a maximum of preparation time and a minimum of cooking time. Time-consuming details can be dealt with the morning of your dinner party, or even the night before. The slow-cooked dishes keep very well, and can be prepared ahead of time. Most important, your menu should be well thought-out, and the ingredients organized and readily accessible.

At the informal Chinese meal, all the dishes are brought to the table at once, and everyone helps himself. The host and/or hostess is free to enjoy being and eating with the guests. This buffetlike approach to food and serving requires that each dish have an individual taste and texture; naturally, no flavor should be repeated. To achieve this, as well as maximum "eye appeal," the Chinese cook dices all the ingredients of one dish, cubes those of a second, and shreds the third.

The possible combinations of flavors are, of course, endless; all can be—and usually are—included in the same meal. Seafood, poultry, beef, and pork—each is prepared in a unique way, and each contributes a special blend to the meal.

After deciding on the number of dishes to be served (determined largely by the number of people who will be eating) and having selected the recipes, read each one carefully, checking the Glossary for any unfamiliar terms or ingredients.

Your menu will probably include one or two slow-cooked meat or poultry dishes, a vegetable dish, a stir-fry, and a soup. (The Chinese serve and sip soup throughout the meal rather than as a first course.) Naturally, there will be rice. Rice is a staple in family-style dining, and is served in separate bowls to each person; the supply is replenished as required. Since most Chinese food is highly seasoned, a function of the rice is to absorb that spiciness, without losing any of the flavor.

Chinese meals seldom are followed by rich desserts, which usually are served only on special feast days, or at banquets. However, even the simplest meal can be turned into a special occasion if the hostess cares to indulge her guests with a Peking Dust or Honeyed Apples. Otherwise, fresh melon or fruit acts as a refreshing finale to the meal.

"Tea" is the first word most Westerners associate with China, and the connection is well-founded. Since approximately 350 B.C., the Chinese have been brewing and enjoying tea for its flavor and fragrance, and for its properties of promoting conversation and sociability.

The centuries have not diminished the Chinese people's love—perhaps need—for tea, nor have they changed their methods of preparing it. Connoisseurs will argue over the exact temperature of the water, the type of vessel to be used, and the length of steeping time, but most Chinese simply put the leaves into a pot (clay or porcelain, never metal) and pour boiling water over them. After a brief interval, the tea is drunk—without milk, lemon, or sugar (except in the South, where milk is sometimes added).

Usually, tea is not served during the meal, as there is a soup or two on the table from which the diners help themselves when they feel thirsty. Tea is reserved for the end of the meal.

There are three basic types of tea: green, black (called "red" by the Chinese), and oolong. All teas come from the same kind of plant; the treatment of the leaves makes the difference in flavor. Leaves that are quickly dried in the sun, then packaged or sold loose, are classified as green tea. Because they retain their natural color, they allegedly produce the most natural flavor. It's the strongest of the teas, and should be used sparingly.

Black tea leaves have been dried and treated to a period of fermentation, during which they turn a dark, coppery color (or "red"). This tea produces a more pungent flavor. Oolong is a pleasant blend of the best of the other two—not as natural as the green, nor as fully fermented as the black. Among the Chinese, it is probably the favorite. But any of the teas whose flavor suits you best is the one to use.

Wine made from grapes is not a natural product of China and, therefore, has no traditional role. Rice wine, however, has been produced for centuries and, in China, the people still drink it with their meals.

The natural sweetness of Chinese food constitutes somewhat of a problem in terms of suitable companion wines. Even the best dry wine can take on a vinegary taste when served with a sweet food. However, there are many light, slightly sweet, or medium dry wines that will complement any Chinese meal. Try serving a sauterne, a dry chablis, Asti Spumanti (called the champagne of Italian wines), or a *vin rosé*. Of course, French or domestic champagne is always right, and can be served throughout the meal. A light American or Japanese beer is also excellent with Chinese food, as is sake served slightly warm.

On the following pages are sample luncheon menus serving 4–5 and sample dinner menus serving 6–8. These menus, some more complex than others, were made entirely from recipes in this book and will make an excellent guide for your adventure into the world of Chinese cooking.

GREEN AND WHITE SOUP
TIP-OUT STEAMED PORK
BEEF FRITTERS
SOUR AND SWEET CABBAGE
GARNISHED STEAMED SOLE
Sauterne

❦

SHAO HSING SOUP
STEAMED BEEF IN RICE FLOUR
SCRAMBLE-FRIED SLICED LAMB
BRAISED TRIPLE WHITE
DOUBLE-FRIED EEL
Rosé

❦

TRIPE SOUP
QUICK-FRIED PORK KIDNEYS
ANCHOVY PORK
BRAISED BEEF WITH TOMATO
CLEAR-STEAMED FISH
SCRAMBLED OMELET
Sake

❦

CHICKEN VELVET AND CORN SOUP
HOT-FRIED KIDNEYS
PEPPERED CHICKEN
BAMBOO SHOOTS IN CHICKEN CREAM
SHRIMP-TOPPED PORK
Light Beer

❦

SQUIRREL FISH
STEAMED PORK WITH SALTED CABBAGE
DOUBLE-FRIED HONEYED LAMB
FISH "EATS" LAMB
RIOT OF SPRING
Dry Chablis

HOT AND SOUR SOUP
STEAMED RICE-PORK PEARLS
BEAN SPROUTS WITH SHREDDED PORK
RED-COOKED SHAD
Dry Chablis

❦

TOMATO AND BEEF BROTH
DEEP-FRIED LAMINATED PORK
MEAT-FILLED MUSHROOMS
LONG-SIMMERED BEEF
VEGETABLE RICE
Light Beer

❦

SWALLOW-SKIN SOUP
AROMATIC AND CRISP CHICKEN
PORK OF FOUR HAPPINESSES
BRAISED BEEF WITH TOMATO
SOLE IN CABBAGE HEARTS
Asti Spumanti

❦

DEEP-FRIED FISH IN WINE-SEDIMENT PASTE
HOT-BRAISED SLICED BEEF
RED-COOKED PORK WITH CHESTNUTS
FRIED FISH STRIPS
Light Beer

❦

CREAM OF CHINESE CABBAGE SOUP
AROMATIC AND CRISP CHICKEN
QUICK-FRIED PORK KIDNEYS
BEEF FRITTERS
RED-COOKED SHAD
Sake

Dinner Menus

SOOCHOW MELON CHICKEN
SWEET AND SOUR CARP
FRIED BAMBOO SHOOTS WITH PICKLED CABBAGE
HAM IN HONEY SAUCE
DOUBLE-COOKED PORK
PEKING DUST
Asti Spumanti

❧

ROYAL CONCUBINE CHICKEN
SOFT-FRIED CRABMEAT
SCRAMBLE-FRIED SLICED LAMB
DRY-FRIED SHRIMP
RIOT OF SPRING
Rosé

❧

SOOCHOW MELON CHICKEN
DOUBLE-FRIED EEL
PORK OF FOUR HAPPINESSES
LONG-SIMMERED BEEF
DRY-FRIED SHRIMP
SQUIRREL FISH
Light Beer

❧

DEEP-FRIED FISH IN WINE-SEDIMENT PASTE
CLAMS IN CHICKEN BROTH
PINE-FLOWER OMELET
QUICK-FRIED CHICKEN
TRIPE SOUP
Asti Spumanti

❧

SPARERIBS AND WATER CHESTNUTS
CANNON-CRACKER CHICKEN
FRY-BRAISED FISH BALLS
SPINACH BALLS
VELVET OF CHICKEN IN BEAN-FLOWER SOUP
Sake

CHICKEN BUNDLES
CREAM OF CHINESE CABBAGE SOUP
FRY-BRAISED FISH BALLS
QUICK-FRIED PORK KIDNEYS
HONEYED APPLES
Sauterne

❧

PORK KIDNEYS IN SESAME JAM
SOY-BRAISED FISH
DEEP-FRIED LAMB
CORAL CABBAGE
WON TON SOUP WITH BAMBOO SHOOTS
Sake

❧

DRUNKEN CHOPS
FISH-BROTH HOT POT
FISH "EATS" LAMB
TARTARS' BARBECUED MEAT
PEPPERED CHICKEN
SWALLOW-SKIN SOUP
Dry Chablis

❧

DRY-FRIED SHRIMP
STEAMED PORK CHOPS WITH PLUMS
QUICK-FRIED CHICKEN
CRYSTAL CHICKEN
CLEAR-STEAMED FISH
DEEP-FRIED FISH IN WINE-SEDIMENT PASTE
Light Beer

❧

CANTONESE CHICKEN, HAM, AND LIVER
SLICED STEAK IN OYSTER SAUCE
SOFT-FRIED CRABMEAT
STEAMED PORK WITH PICKLED CABBAGE
CREAM OF CHINESE CABBAGE SOUP
Dry Chablis

Guide to Dining Out

To the Western mind, China is a land of mystery—and to many Americans, the greatest mystery of all is how those billions of Chinese people manage to live on a diet of chop suey and egg rolls. The answer, of course, is that they don't.

Although most American cities—even the smallest towns—have at least one Chinese restaurant, in all likelihood it has a fairly Americanized menu. The average American has virtually no idea of what the Chinese eat, and because the two cultures differ so drastically, the Chinese tend to believe that Americans would neither understand nor appreciate most of their imaginative, esthetically pleasing specialties.

If you want to expand your expertise as a gourmet, but are limited to dining in a Chinese-American restaurant, ideally you should try to solicit the sympathy of the Chinese proprietor and hope for an invitation to dine with him at his table. In larger cities like New York and San Francisco, the Chinese population is substantial and the Chinese restaurants offer unlimited opportunities to explore every regional specialty.

Open-mindedness is a must for anyone who wishes to fully savor and enjoy Chinese food. Snails in wine-sediment paste, Cannon-Cracker Chicken, Pork of Original Preciousness—unfamiliar names and, perhaps, to the non-Oriental, unlikely things to eat. If you can convince your waiter that you are sincerely interested and adventurous—and if he makes the offer—let him order for you. The results will be rewarding.

Aside from their regular meals, the Chinese like to have several "small eats" throughout the day. Most Chinatowns have dozens of little eating places, open at various times of day and night, and serving everything from full meals to soup, noodles, or meat-filled buns.

One of the most familiar of these is the noodle shop, which often stays open around the clock. The specialty of these shops is single-dish items, such as rich, hearty soups, chow mein and lo mein, and many other noodle or rice dishes served with a variety of meat and vegetable sauces. Noodle shops are never rated for ambience, but only for good food, fast service, and low prices.

The other popular small-eats place is the coffee shop. Like the Western luncheonette, it has counter service, along with a table or two. Full meals, or even hot foods, are never served; rather, their specialty is flour-based finger foods: meat-filled steamed dumplings, sweet buns, and various pastries, and coffee, a favorite drink of Chinese-Americans.

The most important type of eating place in the community is, of course, the restaurant. Many are predominantly Cantonese, mainly because most of the Chinese who first emigrated to America and established restaurants came from the province of Kwangtung.

However, since increasing numbers of proprietors are hiring chefs from other provinces, more Americans are becoming familiar with the peppery-hot food of Szechwan, the home-style cooking of Hunan, the red-cooked food of Shanghai, and the varieties of seafood recipes that originated in Fukien. In some restaurants, the cooking styles of many provinces are intermingled, and patrons may sample the foods of several regions at a single meal.

No Chinese restaurant should be judged solely by its appearance. Plastic-topped tables and chrome chairs, or bare wood tables that have been scrubbed down with left-over tea, have become familiar fixtures to those who have found favorite out-of-the-way places. When the food is excellent, the surroundings are secondary.

Many of the customs of the Chinese in regard to table manners may seem peculiar to a Westerner, but after analyzing them, he will see their logic. The Chinese holds a bowl of plain rice just below his mouth throughout the meal to catch the delicious drippings from the various dishes he is eating. The rice then takes on all the flavors of the different foods and is much the better for it.

The before-dinner cocktail of the West is unknown in China. Tea is always the first thing served in a Chinese restaurant. It is intended only as a welcome to the patron, to be drunk as the party of diners assembles, or during the exchange of pleasantries and greetings. Once dinner has begun, the tea is put aside and wine is served. The teapot reappears at the end of the meal, when the guests are relaxing and congratulating the host on the excellence of the dinner.

Many home-style Chinese restaurants serve soft drinks (typically American) or beer; occasionally, you may find one with a limited wine cellar. If you would like a particular wine with your dinner, phone in advance to see if it is available.

If you are planning a large family or business dinner at a Chinese restaurant, the banquet manager or owner can be very helpful in arranging a good menu. And he will work with you to keep the cost within your means. Be open to suggestions as to the number of dishes best suited to the size of your group and the types of food to be served. Unless you are an expert in Chinese meal-planning, don't insist on a specific dish if he suggests it may not do as well as another. The Chinese are extremely sensitive to harmonious blending of tastes and textures of food. Follow the advice of the professionals, and you will be sure to enjoy success.

On the following pages we have listed some traditional dishes that can be found on most Chinese menus. Some of them, we are sure, will be familiar to you. Try some that are not!

Dining Out Menu

APPETIZERS

SHRIMP TOAST
*toast spread with spicy
shrimp paste then deep fried*

EGG ROLL
*finely chopped shrimp, meat, and
vegetables wrapped in a thin layer of
dough then deep fried*

STEAMED DUMPLINGS
*spiced ground meat wrapped in dough
then steamed*

SOUPS

HOT AND SOUR SOUP
*shredded pork, chicken, and vegetables
cooked in beef or chicken stock
seasoned with tabasco sauce and
vinegar*

CHINESE CABBAGE SOUP
*bits of cabbage, pork, and ginger
cooked in chicken stock*

SHARK'S FIN SOUP
*Dried shark's fin in a clear broth or
cream sauce*

WONTON SOUP
*shredded meat wrapped in dough and
simmered in clear broth*

SWALLOW-SKIN SOUP
*pork, shrimp, and water chestnuts
wrapped in a dough of finely ground
pork and cornstarch then cooked in
boiling water and served in chicken or
beef broth*

BEEF

FRIED CALVES BRAINS
*batter coated calves brains
fried in hot oil*

RED SIMMERED BEEF TRIPE
*beef tripe cooked in sherry
and soy sauce*

RICE FLOUR BEEF
*ginger spiced beef coated
with rice flour*

HOT-BRAISED SLICED BEEF
*beef cooked with chili peppers and
black beans*

BEEF FRITTERS
crisp-fried marinated beef

LONG-SIMMERED BEEF
*beef cubes simmered with spices until
it is almost a meat jelly*

PORK

STEAMED RICE-PORK PEARLS
*ground pork balls coated
with rice and steamed*

SWEET-AND-SOUR PORK
*pork and vegetables cooked in a sweet
and sour sauce*

TWICE-COOKED PORK
hot and spicy pork, boiled then fried

HONEY-PEAR HAM
sweet and salty ham slices

DEEP-FRIED LAMINATED PORK
*pork tenderloin slices dipped in batter
then deep-fried*

QUICK-FRIED PORK
*diced pork tenderloin coated with
beaten egg then fried very quickly*

RED-COOKED PORK WITH CHESTNUTS
*pork cubes and chestnuts stewed in a
broth flavored with soy sauce*

PORK OF ORIGINAL PRECIOUSNESS
*pork slices fried with spices then
steamed with other flavorings and
served with hard-boiled eggs*

POULTRY

CHICKEN WITH BROWN BEAN SAUCE
hot and spicy deep-fried chicken

CHICKEN WITH PEANUTS
*mildly spiced chicken with mushrooms
and roasted peanuts*

SOOCHOW MELON CHICKEN
whole chicken steamed inside a melon

SWINGING CHICKEN
*spicy chicken flavored
with tangerine peel*

AROMATIC AND CRISP CHICKEN
*a whole chicken marinated with
tangerine peel and ginger then steamed
and deep-fried*

PEKING DUCK
*crisply roasted duck served with
scallions and various sauces*

EIGHT JEWEL DUCK
*steamed duck stuffed with rice, dates,
and nuts*

SEAFOOD

SWEET AND SOUR SHRIMP
*shrimp and vegetables cooked in sweet
and sour sauce*

BUTTERFLY SHRIMP
*batter-dipped fried shrimp with ham
and bacon*

RED STIRRED SHRIMP
*shrimp cooked with ginger
and soy sauce*

SQUIRREL FISH
*a whole deep-fried carp or bass served
with a sauce of mushrooms, bamboo
shoots, onion, and ginger*

LOBSTER CANTONESE
*pieces of lobster cooked in a black
bean, pork, and egg sauce*

FRIED FISH IN VEGETABLES
*deep-fried batter-dipped fish served
with Chinese vegetables*

VEGETABLES

SWEET AND SOUR CABBAGE
*shredded cabbage cooked in sweet
and sour sauce*

FRIED BEAN CURD
*cubes of bean curd
quick-fried in oil*

STIR-FRIED MIXED VEGETABLES
*a variety of Chinese vegetables fried
very quickly in a small amount of oil*

STEAMED ASPAGAGUS
*steamed asparagus tips seasoned with
sesame seeds*

RED IN SNOW
fresh peas with salted mustard greens

RICE

PORK FRIED RICE
*steamed rice fried with bits
of pork and vegetables*

CONGEE
*rice cooked to a thin, gruel-like
consistancy*

STEAMED RICE
rice cooked in steam

BOILED RICE
rice cooked in water

NOODLES

CHOW MEIN
*crisp stir-fried noodles with beef, pork,
shrimp, or chicken, and Chinese
vegetables*

ROAST PORK LO MEIN
soft stir-fried noodles with roast pork

SOY JAM NOODLES
*soft noodles with soy jam and
assorted accompaniments*

EGGS

EGG FU YUNG
*Omelet filled with meat and vegetables
and served with a cream sauce*

IRON-POT EGGS
Soufflé with meat and soy sauce

SALTY DUCK EGGS
*aged, hard-boiled eggs served
with congee*

RED-COOKED EGGS
*hard-boiled eggs simmered
in spicy beef broth*

DESSERTS

HONEYED APPLES
*deep-fried batter-coated apple slices
dipped in syrup and sesame seeds*

ALMOND JUNKET
almond flavored sweet custard

PEKING DUST
Pureed chestnuts with whipped cream

Index

Those entries which appear in SMALL CAPITAL LETTERS are the Chinese recipe titles. Roman numbers refer to recipes, *italic numbers* to the text.

Illustrations and Photographs